FIVE ONE-ACT PLAYS

John Bull's Other Isl.

The Canavans (Lady Greg.

Deirdre of the Sorrows - Synge

The Words Upon the Window Pain-
                                Yeats

Lala Noo - Sack B Yeats

in the Traine - O'Connor

Purple dust.

FIVE
ONE-ACT PLAYS

BY

SEAN O'CASEY

THE END OF THE BEGINNING
A POUND ON DEMAND
HALL OF HEALING
BEDTIME STORY
TIME TO GO

MACMILLAN
London · Melbourne · Toronto

ST MARTIN'S PRESS
New York
1966

MACMILLAN AND COMPANY LIMITED
Little Essex Street London WC 2
also Bombay Calcutta Madras Melbourne

THE MACMILLAN COMPANY OF CANADA LIMITED
70 Bond Street Toronto 2

ST MARTIN'S PRESS INC
175 Fifth Avenue New York NY 10010

First issued in St Martin's Library 1958
Reprinted 1962
Reprinted in Pocket Papermacs 1966

PRINTED IN GREAT BRITAIN

CONTENTS

The terms for performance of these plays may be obtained from the League of Dramatists, 84, Drayton Gardens, London, S.W.10, to whom all applications for permission should be made.

THE END OF THE BEGINNING
A Comedy in One Act

CHARACTERS IN THE PLAY

DARRY BERRILL. *About fifty-five; stocky, obstinate, with a pretty big belly. He is completely bald, except for a tuft of grey hair just above the forehead.*

BARRY DERRILL, *Darry's neighbour. Same age as Darry. Thin, easy-going, big moustache, and is very near-sighted.*

LIZZIE BERRILL, *Darry's wife. About forty-five. A good woman about the house, but that's about all.*

A big, comfortable kitchen. Steep stairs, almost like a ladder, leading to upper room, top right. Huge fireplace, right. Some chairs, one heavy, with rubbered castors. Small settee, and table. Chest of drawers, left, on top of which stands a gramophone. Door back, and to left of door a window. To right of door, a dresser, on which is, as well as delf, a large clock of the alarm type. To right of dresser, on a nail, hangs a whip; to the left of dresser hangs a mandolin. On table, a quantity of unwashed delf. To right of fireplace, a lumber room. The room, at night, is lighted by an electric bulb, hanging from centre of ceiling. It is a fine early autumn evening, with the sun low in the heavens. On wall, back, a large red card on which 'Do It Now' is written in white letters. A sink under the window.

Darry (at door of room below. He is shaving, and his chin is covered with lather). This shaving water's dead cold, woman. D'ye hear me? This shaving water's dead cold.

Lizzie (busy about the room — quietly). Come down and heat it, then.

Darry (scornfully). Too much to do, I suppose. I'd do all that has to be done here, three times over, 'n when all was finished, I'd be sighing for something to do.

Lizzie. If you had half of what I have to do here, at the end of the evening you'd be picked up dead out of the debris.

Darry. I would?

Lizzie. You would.

Darry. Sure?

Lizzie. Certain.

9

Darry. If I only had half to do?

Lizzie. Or less.

Darry. I'd be picked up out of the debris?

Lizzie. Out of the middle of it.

Darry. Dead?

Lizzie. As a mackerel.

Darry (fiercely). I'm always challenging you to change places for a few hours, but you won't do it. I'd show you what a sinecure of a job you had here, while I'm sweating out in the fields.

Lizzie. Go out 'n finish the mowing of the meadow. It'll take you only half an hour or so, 'n there's plenty of light in the sky still.

Darry (who has been shaving himself during this argument). The meadow 'll do to be done to-morrow. Why don't you let me do what's to be done in the house, an' you go 'n mow the meadow? Why don't you do that? 'don't you do that? 'you do that? Agony to look at you; agony to listen to you; agony, agony to be anywhere near you.

Lizzie. I'd just like to see you doing what's to be done about the house — I'd just like to see you.

Darry. What is there to be done about the house — will you tell us that?

Lizzie. There's the pig 'n the heifer 'n the hens to be fed 'n tended. There's ironing, cooking, washing, 'n sewing to be done.

Darry. Sewing! An' only a button back 'n front of me so that it's next thing to a miracle that my trousers are kept from starting the neighbours talking.

Lizzie. If you say much more, I'll go 'n mow the meadow, 'n leave you to see what you can make of the house-work.

Darry (*angrily*). Buzz off, buzz off, then, and I'll show you how the work of a house is done. Done quietly; done with speed, 'n without a whisper of fuss in its doing. Buzz off, if you want to, 'n I'll show you 'n all your sex how the work of a house is done!

[*Lizzie violently pulls off a jazz-coloured overall she is wearing, and flings it on the floor.*

Lizzie (*furiously*). Put that on you, 'n do what remains to be done about the house, while I go an' mow the meadow. Get into it, 'n show the world an' your poor wife the wonders you can do when you're under a woman's overall.

Darry (*a little frightened*). Oh, I'll manage all right.

Lizzie. An' don't you let that Alice Lanigan in here while I'm away either, d'ye hear?

Darry. What Alice Lanigan?

Lizzie (*in a temper*). What Alice Lanigan! The Alice Lanigan I caught you chattering to yesterday, when you should have been mowing the meadow. The Alice Lanigan that's setting you on to nag at me about the little I have to do in the house. The Alice Lanigan that's goading you into the idea that if you were a little slimmer round the belly, you'd be a shevaleer, an's getting you to do physical jerks. The Alice Lanigan that's on the margin of fifty, 'n assembles herself together as if she was a girl in her teens, jutting out her bust when she's coming in, 'n jutting out her behind when she's going out, like the Lady of Shalott, to catch the men — that's the Alice Lanigan I mean.

Darry. I don't be thinking of Alice Lanigan.

Lizzie. I've seen you, when you thought I slumbered 'n slept, naked, with nothing at all on you, doing your physical jerks in front of the looking-glass, 'n that, too, when the lessons of a Mission were still hot in your heart — an' all for Alice Lanigan. Maybe you don't know that she has a kid who has never had a pat on the head from a father.

Darry. You buzz off now, 'n I'll show how the work of a house is done.

Lizzie (while she is putting a broad-brimmed hat on her head, pulling a pair of old gloves over her hands, and taking down a whip hanging from a nail in the wall). I'm telling you it's a dangerous thing to shake hands with Alice Lanigan, even with a priest giving the introduction. The day'll come soon when you'll know she's making mechanical toys of you 'n that other old fool, Barry Derrill, who's so near-sighted that he can't see the sky, unless the moon's shining in it!

Darry. Cheerio.

Lizzie (at the door). I'm going now, 'n we'll see how you do the work of the house.

Darry. Hail 'n farewell to you. An' mind you, this'll be only the beginning of things.

Lizzie. God grant that it won't be the end, an' that when I come back, I'll at least find the four walls standing.

> [*She goes out. Darry strolls to the door, and watches her going down the road.*

Darry (scornfully to himself). Mow the meadow! Well, let her see her folly out.

> [*As he shuts the door, the clock in the distant Town Hall strikes eight. Darry returns, glances at the clock on the dresser, notices that it has stopped, takes it up, puts his ear against it, shakes it, begins to wind it, finds it difficult to turn, puts added strength into the turning, and a whirring rattle, like a strong spring breaking, comes from the inside of the clock. He hastily replaces*

the clock on the dresser. After a few seconds' thought, he takes it up again, removes the back, and part of a big, broken spring darts out, which he hurriedly crams in again, and puts the clock back on the dresser.

Darry. Lizzie again!

[*He catches sight of the gramophone, looks at it, thinks for a second, goes over to the chest of drawers, takes some records from behind it, and fixes one on the disc of the gramophone. He takes off his waistcoat, loosens his braces, stands stiff, strokes his thighs, pats his belly, and tries to push it back a little. He starts the gramophone going, runs to the centre of the room, and lies down on the broad of his back. The gramophone begins to give directions for physical exercises, to which Darry listens and, awkwardly, clumsily, and puffingly, tries to follow the movements detailed in the words spoken by the gramophone when the music commences.*

Gramophone. Lie on back; hands behind the head; feet together — are you ready? Bend the right knee; draw it into the waistline, towards the chest — commence!

[*Darry is too slow, or the gramophone is too quick, for he can't keep up with the time of the music. When he finds that he is behind the time of the music, Darry increases his speed by partial performance of the movements, and so gets into touch with the time, but presently, blowing and panting, he is out of time again by a beat or two. He climbs stiffly on to his feet, goes over to gramophone, and puts the indicator to 'Slow'.*

Darry. Phuh. Too quick, too damn quick altogether.

[*He starts the gramophone going, runs to the centre of the room, and again lies down on the broad of his back. When the music begins he goes through the movements as before; but the music is playing so slowly now that he finds it impossible to go slowly enough to keep to the time of the tune. When he finds himself in front of a beat, he stops and puffs and waits for the beat to catch up with him before he recommences. As he is going through these movements, the door opens, and Barry Derrill comes into the room. He has a mandolin under his arm, and is wearing wide-rimmed, thick-lensed spectacles.*

Barry (*briskly*). Come 'n kiss me, sweet 'n twenty — what the hell are you trying to do?

Darry. Can't you see what I'm trying to do? Take off your spectacles 'n get a closer look. Keeping meself fit 'n flexible — that's what I'm trying to do.

Barry. The rhythm's too slow, man; tense your muscles; you're not tun'd into the movements properly, man.

Darry. The indicator must have shifted. Slip over 'n put it to the point marked medium, 'n then get down here 'n give us a hand.

Barry. What about the prologue of playing the song we're to sing at the Town Hall concert?

Darry. Get down 'n have five minutes of this, first; we'll both sing the better for it.

Barry (*dubiously*). Never done it to music, 'n I wouldn't be able to keep in touch with the — with the measure.

Darry. The music makes it easier, man. Keep your eye on me, 'n move when I move.

[*Barry reluctantly takes off his coat and waistcoat, goes over to the gramophone, puts his nose against the instrument, and puts the indicator to 'Fast'.*

Darry. To do this thing properly you'd want to be wearing shorts. Right; now keep in touch with the rhythm, or you'll mar everything. Start her off, and stretch yourself down.

> [*Barry starts the gramophone, runs over and lies down opposite to Darry, so that the soles of their feet are only a few inches apart.*

Gramophone (*very rapidly*). Lie on back; hands behind the head; feet together — are you ready? Bend the right knee; draw it into the waistline towards the chest; breathe out — commence!

> [*The tempo of the tune forces them to do the exercises in a frantic way, till it dawns on Darry, who is nearly exhausted, that there's something wrong. He stops while Barry goes on manfully.*

Darry (*scornfully*). Eh, eh, there, wait a minute, wait a minute, man. Don't you see anything wrong?

Barry (*stopping*). No; what's wrong?

Darry (*testily*). Aw, what's wrong! We're congestin' ourselves with speed; that's what's wrong. You must have jammed the indicator hard to Fast. (*He gets up, goes to the gramophone, and puts it right.*) We're entertainin' ourselves, an' not tryin' to say the Rosary.

> [*He comes back and stretches himself again on the floor. The music begins and the two men commence the exercises. After a few moments, Darry slows down a little, misses several beats, and tries to blame Barry.*

Darry (*excitedly keeping up the movements, but out of time, as he talks*). Try to keep the proper rhythm up, man. (*He hums the tune of 'Coming thro' the Rye'.*) Dad th' didee dah th' diddy dah th' diddy dee — that way, man. Dah th' diddy dah th' diddy (*rapidly*). Keep your eye on me. Dah th' diddy dee.

[*After a few moments Darry is out of time and breathless; he stops and sits up to complain, but he really wants to get a rest.*

Darry (*with aggravated patience*). Barry, you're spoiling the whole thing by getting out of time. Don't let your arms and legs go limber, tense your muscles. Three beats to the bar, see? Now!

[*They start again; Darry is soon behind time, blowing and puffing out of him. Barry keeps to the beat of the tune splendidly.*

Darry (*angrily*). You're going too damn quick altogether, now, man!

Barry. No I'm not — I'm there to the tick every time.

Darry (*violently*). There to the tick — how is it you're not in the line with me, then, if you're there to the tick? I don't know whether you're in front of me or behind me. Are you too stiff or what?

Barry. I'm there to the second every time. It's you that's missin' a beat in the bar.

Darry (*indignantly, stopping to talk, while Barry goes on*). I'm missin' it because I'm trying to foster you into the right balance 'n rhythm of the movements. That's why I'm missin' it. (*Loudly*) An' I'm wastin' me time!

Barry (*sharply*). I'm doing me best, amn't I?

Darry (*more sharply still*). Your best's a hell of a way behind what's wanted. It's pitiful 'n painful to be watchin' you, man. (*He stands up and looks at Barry, who keeps going.*) Eh, eh, you'll do yourself an injury, Barry. Get up 'n we'll do the song. (*As Barry goes on*) Oh, get up 'n we'll do the song.

[*Barry gets up reluctantly, and Darry goes over and stops the gramophone.*

Barry. I was doin' it well enough, if you'd let me alone.

Darry (scornfully). Yes; like the Londonderry Air play'd in march time.

[*They get their mandolins and stand side by side at the back.*

Darry. Now we walk in a semicircle down to the front, 'n bow, you remember? Ready?

Barry. Yep.

Darry. Go!

[*They both step off to the right, take a few steps, and then they halt.*

Barry. Something wrong; we don't go round the same way, do we?

Darry (testily). Of course there's something wrong; of course we don't go round the same way. Can't you try to remember, Barry? You're to go to the left, to the left.

Barry. I remember distinctly I was to go to the right.

Darry (irritably). Oh, don't be such an egotist, Barry. Now think for a minute (*A pause.*) Now make up your mind — d'ye want to go to the left or the right?

Barry (testily). Oh, left, right — any way.

Darry. Left, then. Go.

[*They march round, one to the right, the other to the left, meet in the front, and bow.*

Darry. You start, Barry, my boy.

Barry (singing).

One summer eve a handsome man met a handsome maiden strolling,

Darry.

Down where the bees were hummin' an' the wild flowers gaily growing;

Barry.

Said she, We'll sit down here a while, all selfish thoughts controlling,

Darry.

Down where the bees are hummin' an' the wild flowers gaily growing:

Barry.

Said she, We'll meditate on things, things high 'n edifying,

How all things live 'n have their day 'n end their day by dying.

He put his hand on her white breast an' murmur'd, Life is trying,

Darry.

Down where the bees are hummin' an' the wild flowers gaily growing.

Barry.

The moon glanc'd down 'n wonder'd what the pair of them were doing,

Darry.

Down where the bees were hummin' an' the wild flowers gaily growing;

Barry.

Then th' moon murmur'd, I feel hot, 'n fear a storm is brewing,

Darry.

Down where the bees are hummin' an' the wild flowers gaily growing.

Barry.

She talk'd so well of things so high, he started to reward
  her,

The moon ran in behind a cloud, for there was none to
  guard her.

I'll take that off, she said, you'd ruin the lace that's round
  the border,

Darry.

Down where the bees are hummin' an' the wild flowers
  gaily growing.

Barry.

White-featur'd 'n thin goodie-goodies rush around
  excited,

Darry.

Down where the bees are hummin' an' the wild flowers
  gaily growing;

Barry.

Proclaiming that the dignity of living has been blighted,

Darry.

Down where the bees are hummin' an' the wild flowers
  gaily growing.

Barry.

But when the light is soft 'n dim, discovery disarming,

The modest moon behind the clouds, young maidens, coy
  'n charming,

Still cuddle men who cuddle them, 'n carry on alarming,

Darry.

Down where the bees are hummin' an' the wild flowers
  gaily growing.

[*When the song has ended, Darry cocks his ear and listens.*

Barry. Shall we try it once more?

Darry. Shush, shut up, can't you?

> [*Darry goes over to the door, opens it, and listens intently. There is heard the rattling whirr caused by the steady and regular movement of a mowing machine. The distant Town Hall clock strikes nine.*

Darry (hastily putting the mandolin away). I forgot. I'll have to get going.

Barry. Get going at what?

Darry. House-work. (*He begins to get into the overall left off by Lizzie.*) I dared her, an' she left me to do the work of the house while she was mowing the meadow. If it isn't done when she comes back, then sweet good-bye to the status I had in the home. (*He finds it difficult to get the overall on.*) Dih dih dih, where's the back 'n where's the front, 'n which is which is the bottom 'n which is the top?

Barry. Take it quietly, take it quietly, Darry.

Darry (resentfully). Take it quietly? An' the time galloping by? I can't stand up on a chair 'n say to the sun, stand thou still there, over the meadow th' missus is mowing, can I?

Barry. I know damn well you can't, but you're not going to expedite matters by rushing around in a hurry.

Darry (he has struggled into the overall). Expedite matters! It doesn't seem to strike you that when you do things quickly, things are quickly done. Expedite matters! I suppose loitering to look at you lying on the broad of your back, jiggling your legs about, was one way of expediting matters; an' listening to you plucking curious sounds out of a mandolin, an' singing a questionable song, was another way of expediting matters?

Barry. You pioneered me into doing two of them yourself.

Darry (busy with the pot on the fire). I pioneered you into doing them! Barry Derrill, there's such a thing in the world as a libel. You came strutting in with a mandolin under your arm, didn't you?

Barry. I did, but——

Darry. An' you sang your song.

Barry. Yes, but——

Darry. When you waltz'd in, I was doing callisthenics, wasn't I?

Barry. I know you were; but all the same——

Darry. An' you flung yourself down on the floor, and got yourself into a tangle trying to do them too, didn't you?

Barry. Hold on a second——

Darry. Now, I can't carry the conversation into a debate, for I have to get going. So if you can't give a hand, go, 'n let me do the things that have to be done, in an orderly 'n quiet way.

Barry. 'Course I'll give a hand — only waiting to be asked.

Darry (*looking at the clock, suddenly*). Is the clock stopped?

Barry (*taking up clock and putting it close to his ear*). There's no ticking, 'n it's hours slow.

Darry. Lizzie again! Forgot to wind it. Give the key a few turns, Barry, an' put the hands on to half-past nine.

> [*Barry starts to wind the clock. Darry goes over to table, gets a basin of water, begins to wash the delf, humming to himself the air of the song, 'Down where the bees are humming'. Barry winds and winds away, but no sign is given of a tightening of the spring inside. He looks puzzled, winds again, and is about to silently put the clock back where he found it, when Darry turns and looks at him questioningly.*

Darry. You've broken the damn thing, have you?

Barry. I didn't touch it.

Darry. Didn't touch it? Amn't I after looking at you twisting an' tearing at it for nearly an hour? (*He comes over to Barry.*) Show me that. (*He takes the clock from Barry and opens the back, and the spring darts out.*) Didn't touch it. Oh, for God's sake be more careful when you're handling things in this house! Dih dih dih. (*He pushes the spring back, and slaps the clock down on the dresser.*) You must have the hands of a gorilla, man. Here, come over 'n wipe while I wash.

> [*A slight pause while the two of them work at the delf. Darry anxiously watches Barry, who, being very near-sighted, holds everything he wipes close up to his spectacles.*

Darry (*suddenly*). Look out, look out, there — you're not leaving that jug on the table at all; you're depositing it in the air, man!

Barry (*peering down at the table*). Am I? Don't be afraid, I won't let anything drop.

Darry (*humming the song*). Dum dah de de dum da dee dee dum dah dee dee dee dah ah dum.

Barry (*swinging his arm to the tune*). Down where the bees are hummin' an' the wild flowers gaily growing.

Darry. Fine swing, you know. Dum dah dee dee dum dah dee dee dum dah dee dee dee dah ah dum.

Barry (*swinging his arm*). Down where the bees are hummin' —

> [*Barry's arm sends the jug flying off the table on to the floor.*

Darry (*yelling*). You snaky-arm'd candle-power-ey'd elephant, look at what you're after doing!

Barry (*heatedly*). It's only a tiny jug, anyhow, 'n you can hardly see the pieces on the floor!

Darry (just as heatedly). An' if I let you do much more, they would soon be big enough to bury us! Sit down, sit down in the corner there; do nothing, say nothing, an', if I could, I'd put a safety curtain round you. For God's sake, touch nothing while I run out an' give the spuds to the pig.

> [*Darry dashes over to the fire, whips the pot off, and runs out. He leaves the door open, and again the rattling whirr of a mowing machine can be heard. Barry sits dejectedly in a corner. After a few moments a bump is heard outside, followed by a yell from Darry, who, a second later, comes rushing madly in, a bloody handkerchief pressed to his nose. He flings himself flat on the floor on his back, elevating his nose as much as possible.*

Darry. Get me something cold to put down the back of my neck, quick!

Barry (frightened). What the hell did you do to yourself?

Darry. I didn't bend low enough when I was going in, 'n I gave myself such a — oh, such a bang on my nose on the concrete. Get something cold, man, to shove down the back of my neck 'n stop the bleeding!

Barry. Keep the nose sticking up in the air as high as you can. I don't know where to get something cold to shove down the back of your neck. I knew this rushing round wouldn't expedite matters.

Darry (with a moan of resentment as he hears 'expedite matters'). Oh, pull yourself together, man, 'n remember we're in the middle of an emergency.

Barry. A little block of ice, now, would come in handy.

Darry. A little — oh, a little block of ice! An' will you tell us where you're going to get a little block of ice? An', even if we had one, how could you fasten it down the back of my neck?

Eh? Can't you answer — where are you going to get a block of ice?

Barry. How the hell do I know where I'm going to get it?

Darry. D'ye expect me to keep lying here till the winter comes?

> [*During this dialogue Barry is moving round the room aimlessly, peering into drawers, rattling the delf on the dresser with his nose as he looks along the shelves.*

Darry (*as he hears the crockery rattling*). Mind, mind, or you'll break something. I must be losing a lot of blood, Barry, an' I won't be able to keep my nose sticking up in the air much longer. Can't you find anything?

Barry. I can see nothing.

Darry. Run upstairs 'n get the key of the big shed that's hanging on the wall, somewhere over the mantelpiece at the far end of the room. Go quick, man!

> [*Barry runs upstairs, goes into room, comes out again, and looks down at Darry.*

Darry (*up to him*). Did you get it?

Barry. Where's the switch? It's as dark as pitch in there.

> [*Darry, with a moan of exasperation, sits up, but immediately plunges down on his back again.*

Darry. Starts pumping out again the minute I sit up. (*To Barry*) There's no switch in that room. We can't have a switch in every corner of the room just to suit you! You've only got to move down the centre of the room till you come to the fireplace; then brush your hand over the mantelpiece, along the wall, till you feel the key hanging there.

> [*Barry goes back into the room. After a few seconds' silence, there is a crash of falling crockery. Darry, after*

a second of silent consternation, sits up with a jerk, but
immediately plunges down on his back again.

Darry (sinking supine on the floor). What has he done now;
oh, what has he done now? (*Shouting up to Barry*) Eh, you up
there — what have you done now?

Barry (sticking his head out of door above). Nothing much —
the washhand-stand fell over.

Darry (angrily). Nothing much. It sounded a hell of a lot,
then. You're the kind of man if you're not chained up, 'll
pull everything in the house asundher! Come down, come
down, 'n stop down, or that delicate little hand of yours 'll
smash everything in the house!

Barry. My eyes are used to the darkness, now, 'n I can see.
I'll get the key for you.

[*He goes back into the room, leaving Darry speechless.*
After a few seconds, he comes out of the room in a sweat
of fright and anger, one hand tightly clasped over the
other. He rushes down the stairs, and begins to pull the
things out of the chest of drawers, every other moment
leaving off to clasp one hand over the other.

Barry (frantically). Get your own key, get your own key.
Half slaughtering myself for your sake! Why don't you keep
your razor-blades in a safe place, an' not leave them scattered
about in heaps all over the mantelpiece? Where is there a bit
of old rag till I bind up my wounds? Get your own key yourself, I'm tellin' you.

Darry. Amn't I nicely handicapped, wanting help an' having
only the help of a half-blind man?

Barry. D'ye know I'm nearly after mowing my fingers off
with your blasted razor-blades? (*Coming near to Darry, with a*
handkerchief in his hand, and showing the injured fingers to him)

Look at them, uh, look at them — one looks as if only a thin thread of flesh was keeping it on. How am I going to play the mandolin now?

Darry. You'd play it better if all your fingers were off.

Barry (keeping the wounded hand in the air, and holding out the handkerchief to Darry with the other). Here, get a grip of this 'n help me to bind up me wounds.

> [*Barry kneels down beside the prostrate Darry, who takes the handkerchief and proceeds to tie it round Barry's wounded fingers.*

Darry (keeping his nose well up in the air). You give that an unexpected honour, if you call that a wound!

> [*Darry ties the handkerchief round Barry's hand, who stands looking at it.*

Barry (reflectively). Won't be able to do much for you with it now.

Darry. It'll limit your capacity for breakin' things.

> [*A pause.*

Darry. Slip out, Barry, old son, 'n see if the heifer's safe on the bank beside the house.

> [*Barry goes outside the door and stands looking up towards the top of the house. The light has been fading, and it is getting dark. Again can be heard the whirr of the mowing machine, and the Town Hall clock strikes ten.*

Barry. I think I can hear her croppin' the grass all right, but it doesn't seem wise to leave her there 'n the dusk fallin'.

Darry (testily). I can't do anything till this bleeding stops, can I?

Barry. The spuds are all scattered about here where you let them fall when you were runnin' in.

Darry (moaning). 'N can't you get the broom 'n sweep them up into a corner, 'n not be trampling them into the ground; you see the state I'm in!

[*Barry gets the broom and starts to sweep outside the door.*

Barry (in to Darry). How's it now?

Darry (cautiously sitting up). It's nearly stopped now, but I'll have to go cautious.

[*Barry, sweeping with one hand, manages to bring the broom-handle into contact with the window, and breaks a pane. A silent pause.*

Barry (as if he didn't know). What's that, what's that?

Darry (in an agony of anger). What's that, what's that! Can't you see, man, that you're after thrustin' the handle of the broom through one of the windows?

Barry (peering down at the hole in the window). That's curious, now, for I never felt the handle touchin' the window; but there's a hole in it, right enough.

Darry (with angry mockery). No, you wouldn't feel it touchin' it, either. A hole in it — of course there's a hole in it! My God Almighty, I've a destroyin' angel in the house!

Barry. Well, not much use of lookin' at it now.

Darry (vehemently). Oh, come in, come in, come in, man. Didn't you hear the clock strikin' ten? I'll have to get goin' now.

[*He gets up gingerly, feeling his nose, and still keeping it at a high angle.*

Barry (introducing another subject). Hadn't you better stable the heifer before you do anything?

Darry (violently). Haven't I to clean out the cowhouse first before I stable her, man? With your exercisin', 'n your singin', 'n your great 'n godly gift of expeditin' matters, I haven't made a bit of headway! I hadn't a chance to give her the graze she needs, so let her get all she can on the bank at the back of the house.

Barry. Supposing she wanders to the edge of the bank 'n tumbles off?

Darry. I don't know what to do about that.

Barry. Couldn't you tie her to something?

Darry (angrily). There's nothing to tie her to, man.

Barry. What about putting a rope down the chimney 'n tying it to something in the room?

Darry (after a few seconds' thought). That's a good idea, Barry. There's a rope outside, an' I'll sling one end round her neck, let the other end down the chimney, an' tie it to a chair. Wait here a second 'n get it when it comes down.

[*Darry rushes out. After a few moments his voice is heard faintly from above calling 'Hello, hello!' Barry, who has his head a little up the chimney, the smoke making him cough, answers, 'Righto, let her come.' The rope comes down; Barry catches the end and pulls it into the room. Darry returns, and they tie the rope to a chair.*

Barry. Put the chair at the far end of the room, an' if the heifer wanders too far, we'll see the chair moving across the room.

Darry (with enthusiasm). Now you're beginnin' to use your brains at last, Barry, me boy. (*He shifts the chair to the far end of the room.*) Now we can get goin' 'n get everything shipshape before the missus toddles back. Let's put on the light and see what we're doin'.

[*He snaps down the switch, but no light comes into the bulb.*

Darry (annoyed). Dih dih dih — must be the meter again.

[*He hurries into the lumber room, stepping over the rope.*

Barry (*speaking in to Darry*). I wouldn't do much tamperin' with that.

Darry (*inside room — emphatically*). Oh, I know what I'm doin'.

> [*Darry rushes out again, snaps down the switch, but no light comes.*

Darry (*irritably*). Must be the blasted bulb. (*He rushes to a drawer.*) There's a bulb here, somewhere, we've had for a long time, 'n never used. (*He takes one from the drawer.*) Here we are. (*He pulls a chair to the centre of the room, stands on it, takes off the old bulb, and gives it to Barry.*) See if you can see anything wrong with it.

Barry (*holding it to his nose*). Can't see anything.

Darry. Leave it down, leave it down.

Barry. Sure the one you're fixing's the right voltage?

Darry (*stopping to look at Barry*). 'Course it's the right voltage. Why wouldn't it be the right voltage?

Barry. If it wasn't, it might fuse.

Darry. Fuse? No fear of it fusing.

> [*He starts to work again.*
> [*The chair to which the rope is tied begins to move across the floor.*

Barry (*startled*). Look out, look out — the heifer's moving!

Darry. Catch hold of it, catch hold of it, before she disappears up the chimney!

> [*Barry catches the chair, but the strain is too much, and he is pulled along. Darry jumps down off the chair, leaves the bulb on the table, catches hold of the rope, and helps Barry to tug the chair back to the far end of the room.*

Darry. You sit on the chair, 'n then she can't move without our knowledge.

[*Barry sits on the chair; Darry mounts the chair again, and starts to fix the bulb. The chair begins to move with Barry sitting on it.*

Barry (*excitedly*). Eh, quick again, get down, the heifer's movin'!

[*Darry jumps down again, and the two of them pull the chair back to its place.*

Darry. The missus'll be back 'n nothin' done but damage.

[*He gets up again and fixes the bulb; there is a flash, and the room is darker than ever.*

Barry (*like a prophet*). I warned you, Darry; I saw it comin'.

Darry (*forcibly*). What are you blatherin' about? We're no worse off than we were before we fixed it. There's a drum of oil in the lumber room, 'n if there's any left in it we can light the lamps. You light the one hangin' on the wall, while I see how we stand.

[*He runs into the lumber room. Barry takes the lamp from the wall, removes the chimney, and tries to light the wick, but he can't see it, and holds the match anywhere but near the wick. Darry comes out of cellar.*

Darry (*jubilantly*). Plenty of oil in it. Aw, you're not holding the match within a mile of the wick, man. Show it to me, show it to me.

[*He takes the match from Barry, and lights the lamp.*

Darry. Out with you now, 'n get one of the old lamps you'll find on one of the shelves to the right in the shed at the back of the yard.

Barry. How'll I see?

Darry. Strike a match 'n look. You'll see them staring at you. I'll take a canful of oil from the drum to put in it when you bring it back, 'n then we'll have lashin's of light.

Barry (*going out by door*). I know I won't be able to see.

   [*Darry, with a can that has a long snout on it, runs back
   into the lumber room. Barry has left the door open, and
   the rattling whirr of the mowing machine can be heard
   again. There is a slight pause. Suddenly Darry rushes
   out of the lumber room over to the open door.*

Darry (*shouting madly*). Barry, Barry, come here quick,
man! I turned the key of the tap too much, 'n it slipped out of
me hand into a heap of rubbish 'n I can't turn off the cock, 'n
I can't find the key in the dark. Come quick, man, or there
won't be a drop of oil left in the drum!

   [*He rushes wildly back into the lumber room. Another
   slight pause. He rushes out again, with the drum in his
   arms, his thumb pressed to the tap outlet, and runs over
   to the door.*

Darry (*calling madly*). Eh, Barry, Barry, d'ye hear me callin'
you, man? I won't be able to keep this oil in much longer.
Have you fallen asleep or what?

   [*There is heard outside a rattle, followed by a crash of falling pots, tins, and tools; then a dead silence for a moment.*

Darry (*staggering against the wall*). Aw, Mother o' God,
what's he after doin' now!

Barry (*outside, in a loud voice of great distress*). Darry, oh,
Darry, I'm after nearly destroyin' meself! Where's the doorway? — I can't see!

Darry (*going over and standing in the doorway*). Here, here,
man; no, to the left. (*As Barry staggers in, dusty and frightened*)
What ruin are you after causin' now?

Barry (*moaningly*). I'm after gettin' an awful shock!

Darry (*appealingly*). Pull yourself together, for God's sake,
man, 'n tell us what's happened.

Barry (as he sinks down on a chair). The blasted lamps were on top of the top shelf; there was nothing to stand on; I had to climb upon the shelves, and climbing up, the shelves 'n all that was on them came down on top of me!

[*Darry goes over and rests the drum in the sink, his hand still pressed over the outlet of the tap.*

Darry. 'N why did you climb the shelves? What did you want to do that for? Couldn't you see, you sap, that they weren't fixed well in the wall? Why did you insist on climbing the shelves?

Barry. I was just tryin' to expedite matters.

Darry (with a wail). Tryin' to expedite matters. Oh, there'll be a nice panorama of ruin in front of Lizzie when she comes back!

Barry. 'N me spectacles were sent flyin' when the shelves fell.

Darry. 'N why didn't you grab them before they fell to the ground?

Barry (hotly). How could I grab them 'n they fallin', when I was fallin' too!

Darry (impatiently). Well, get the lamp then, 'n look for the lost key in the lumber room.

Barry. 'N maybe let it fall, 'n set the house on fire?

Darry (woefully). Oh, amn't I in a nice predic — The chair, the chair — the heifer's movin'!

[*The chair to which the rope is tied begins to move across the floor. Barry catches it, tugs manfully, but he is carried on towards the fireplace.*

Barry (anxiously). Give us a hand, give us a hand, or I'll be up the chimney!

[*Darry leaving the drum, runs over to Barry's side, grips the rope in front of Barry, and, to get a safer hold, takes the rope off the chair and puts it round him under his arms. With great pulling, they get the rope a little back. The oil flows from the drum into the sink unnoticed.*

Darry (panting). Keep a strain, or we'll be up the chimney!

Barry. How'm I goin' to get home to-night without me spectacles?

Darry (loudly). Keep a sthrain on her, man, keep a sthrain on her; we have to get this straightened out first, before we can brood over your spectacles!

Barry (suddenly noticing the oil drum). The oil, the oil!

[*He lets go of the rope, and runs over to the oil drum. Darry disappears up the chimney.*

Barry (lifting the drum and shaking it). Not a drop left in it, not a single drop! What're we goin' to do n——

[*He turns and sees that Darry has disappeared.*

Lizzie (speaking outside in a voice of horror). The heifer, the heifer!

Darry (calling out). Lizzie, Lizzie!

[*Lizzie rushes in as Darry falls down the chimney. He crawls out from the fireplace on his hands and knees, and halts there, exhausted and sooty.*

Lizzie (horrified). What in the Name of God has happened?

Darry (to Lizzie). Now you see the result of havin' your own way! Why the hell didn't you hold on to the rope when you took it off the heifer, so that I wouldn't come down with a bump?

Lizzie. How'd I know you were hangin' on the other end?

Darry (indignantly). You didn't know — my God, woman, can you do nothin' right!

CURTAIN

DOWN WHERE THE BEES ARE HUMMING

One sum-mer eve a hand-some man met a hand-some maid-en stroll-ing, Down where the bees were hum-ming and the wild flowers gai-ly grow-ing; Said she, We'll sit down here a while, all self-ish thoughts con-troll-ing, Down where the bees are hum-ming and the wild flowers gai-ly grow-ing: Said she, We'll med-i-tate on things, things high and ed-i-fy-ing, How all things live and have their day and end their day by dy-ing. He put his hand on her white breast and mur-mured, Life is try-ing, Down where the bees are hum-ming and the wild flowers gai-ly grow-ing.

A POUND ON DEMAND
A Sketch in One Act

CHARACTERS IN THE PLAY

A GIRL, *in charge of Pimblico Sub-Post Office*
JERRY, *a working man*
SAMMY, *another*
A POLICEMAN

SCENE

A Sub-Post Office on a late autumn evening

A Post Office. There is a counter to the right which comes out for about four yards, turning at right angles, and running to the back. That part of the counter facing front is railed, and has in the centre a small, bracketed window for selling stamps. Above the window is a card on which is the word STAMPS. *There is a swing-door in the centre at the back. To the right of the door a window having the words* POST OFFICE *on it to face towards the street. To the left is a table-ledge for the convenience of those who want to write letters, telegrams, fill in forms, or make out postal orders. Blotting-paper, quill pens, inkwells are on the ledge. Above ledge at back a telephone booth. Notices, such as, Save Saving Certificates and Saving Certificates will Save you; Buy by Telephone; Post often and Post early; Cardinal Virtues: Temperance, Prudence, Fortitude, Payment of Income Tax.*

Behind the counter, sitting on a high stool beside a desk, is a Girl, sorting and examining documents, and doing the routine work of a Post Office. Behind counter, on the left, a door. It is six o'clock or so in the evening of an autumn day; the sun is low in the sky, and his red light is flooding in through the window.

The swing-door suddenly opens and Jerry, pressing his body against the door to keep it open, while he holds Sammy, who is drunk, steady with his right hand, appears to view with an anxious and hopeful look on his face. Jerry is dressed in cement-soiled working clothes, and his trousers are bound under the knees with cords. He is about forty years of age. His friend, Sammy, is a workman too, and is dressed in the same way. Jerry wears a large tweed cap, and Sammy wears a brown trilby much the worse for wear. Sammy is in a state of maudlin drunkenness, and his reddish face is one wide, silly grin.

37

Jerry (*holding on to Sammy and calling in to the Girl*). Yous do Post Office Savin's Bank business here, don't you, miss?

[*Before the Girl has time to reply, Sammy lurches away from the door, pulling Jerry with him, and the door swings shut again. The Girl looks round, but sees only the swinging door. A pause. The door opens again, and Jerry, holding Sammy with a firmer grip, appears and speaks in to the Girl.*

Jerry (*to the Girl*). Savin's Bank's business's's done here, miss, isn't it?

[*Sammy lurches again, pulling Jerry with him, so that the door again swings shut. Again the Girl looks round and sees only the swinging door. She keeps her eyes on it. A pause. The door opens again and the two men appear, this time with Jerry behind Sammy, pushing him, and looking round him as he speaks in to the Girl.*

Jerry (*looking round Sammy as he speaks in to the Girl*). Savin's Bank business's's done here, isn't it, miss?

Girl (*suspiciously*). Yes.

Jerry (*exultantly to Sammy*). I told you, Sammy, this is a Post Office where Savin's Bank business's's done. In we go.

Sammy (*looking round vacantly*). Where?

Jerry. In there, in here, can't you see? We're in port, Sammy — Post Office where Savin's Bank business's's done.

Sammy (*vacantly*). Where?

Jerry (*appealingly*). Aw, pull yourself together, Sammy. Remember the mission we're on; don't let a fella down now. Remember what we want.

Sammy (*vacantly*). Want nothin'.

Jerry (*irritably*).   Try to remember, man — pound on demand — remember?

Sammy (stiffening). Pound on demand, wanna pound on demand.

Jerry. Why're you sayin' you want nothin', then? Don't make a fool of me when it comes to the push. You've only to sign a form — the young lady 'll give it to you.

Sammy. Sign no form; don't wanna form.

Jerry (irritably). You can't get your pound, man, till you sign a form. That's the way they do Savin's Bank business's, see? Sign a form askin' a pound on demand, 'n hand it over to the young lady, see?

Sammy. Wanna drink.

Jerry. You've no money for a dhrink. Can't get a dhrink till you get your pound on demand. (*Guiding Sammy over to the counter.*) Thry to keep your composure while we're doing the business.

[*The pair come to the counter.*

Jerry (in a wheedling way to the Girl). He wants a pound on demand, missie; (*to Sammy*) don't you, Sammy — a pound on demand? (*To the Girl*) Give's the form, missie, till he pops his name down on it.

Girl (to Sammy — ignoring Jerry). What can I do for you, sir?

Sammy (vacantly). Wha'?

[*A stoutish Woman of about forty comes in by the door with a minor kind of a rush, and hurries over to the counter. She stares for a moment at the two men.*

Woman (to the Girl). If I wrote a letter 'n posted it to catch the seven fifty-nine P.M. collection, would it get to Tarraringa-patam on Friday before twelve fifty-four in the afternoon, please?

Girl (*trying to collect her wits together*). What collection, madam?

Woman (*stiffly*). I said the seven fifty-nine P.M. collection, I think.

Jerry (*impatiently*). Gie's the little form, missie.

Sammy (*drunkenly breaking into song*). Jush a song at twilight, when the lights 're slow——

Jerry (*remonstrating*). Eh, eh, there, Sammy!

Sammy (*a little subdued*). 'N the flickerin' shadowish softly——

Jerry (*emphatically*). Eh, Sammy, eh!

Sammy (*ending it softly*). Come 'n go.

Girl (*to the Woman*). The destination of the letter, madam, please?

Woman. Tarraringapatam.

Girl. Where exactly is that place or locality, madam?

Sammy. Nex' parish but one t' ourish.

Woman (*indignantly, to Sammy*). Keep your funny remarks to yourself, please. (*To the Girl*) Tarraringapatam's in the most southern part of Burma.

Jerry (*to the Girl*). Fork over the form for the pound on demand, will you, missie? Before me pal gets too tired to sign.

Girl (*to Jerry*). One minute, please.

Sammy (*hammering on counter with his hand*). A pound en deman', wanna pound en deman'.

Woman (*to the Girl*). Will a letter posted to catch the seven fifty-nine get to Tarraringapatam on Friday before twelve fifty-four in the afternoon?

Girl. I'm afraid I couldn't say, madam.

Jerry (*briskly, to the Woman*). Young lady doesn't know. (*To the Girl*) Pound on demand form, miss.

Woman (*indignantly, to Jerry*). Be good enough, sir, to confine your attention to your own business, will you? (*To the Girl*) Will you find out?

Jerry (*to the Woman*). You can't be let monopolise the time 'n attention of an office for the use of the public at large, can you?

Sammy (*briskly*). Ish she tryin' to shtir up trouble, or wha'?

Woman (*to Sammy*). I'm making an ordinary enquiry at a public office, and I will not tolerate interference.

Girl (*who has been running her finger along a list of names of places hanging on a card behind the counter*). What name, again, please?

Woman (*with dignity*). Tarraringapatam.

Girl (*looking at the list*). Not on the list, madam.

Jerry (*ironically*). Bus stop in the jungle, miss.

Woman. It must be there.

Girl (*to the Woman*). Not on the list. (*To Sammy*) What can I do for you, sir?

Jerry (*confidentially*). Just wants a pound on demand, miss.

Girl (*sharply to Jerry*). Let the gentleman speak for himself. (*To Sammy*) What is it, please?

Sammy. Ish she tryin' to shtir up trouble, or wha'?

Jerry (*loudly, to Sammy*). Young lady's askin' if you want a pound on demand.

Sammy (*wakening up a little*). Yeh, wha'? Wanna pound on demand, yeh.

Jerry (*briskly*). Give's the form, 'n I'll get him to sling his name down, missie.

Girl (*to Sammy*). Can I have your bank-book, please?

Jerry (*briskly*). Bank-book, bank-book, Sammy; young lady wants the bank-book.

[*Sammy looks vacantly at the Girl and at Jerry.*

Jerry (*briskly*). Get a move on. (*He puts a hand in Sammy's breast-pocket.*) Bank-book, bank-book, Sammy, me son; young lady wants bank-book.

[*He takes the book from Sammy's pocket, and hands it to the Girl.*

Girl (*to Woman, who is standing beside the counter*). Sorry, madam, but I can't tell you what you want to know — the name's not on the list. (*She looks at the bank-book Jerry has given to her.*) Which is Mr. Adams?

Jerry (*gaily indicating his friend*). This is him, miss, all alive 'n full of beans.

Sammy (*delightedly*). Jusht a song at twilight when the lights aresh slow——

Jerry (*interrupting*). Shush — young lady doesn't like singing in her office, Sammy.

Sammy (*drunkenly*). Sammy doesn't care about any young ladyish; don't care 'bout offish or young ladyish.

Woman (*going over indignantly to ledge to write her letter*). A finely appointed Post Office, I must say, that can't give you even a hint about the commonest postal regulation!

[*The Girl slowly gets a form and reluctantly hands it out towards Sammy, but Jerry takes it out of her hand, and hurries Sammy over to the writing-ledge opposite.*

Girl (*warningly*). The depositor must sign himself; and his signature must correspond with that in the book.

[*The woman is writing her letter, and is taking up a great deal of space. She is right in the middle of the ledge with*

writing materials spread round on each side of her. Jerry
leads Sammy to the space on her right, looks at it, then
leads Sammy round to the space on her left.

Jerry. Now you've only just to gather the pen into your mit
'n slap down the old name on to the form.

[*Jerry spreads the form on the ledge, gets an old pen and*
puts it into Sammy's hand, who lets it fall to the floor.

Jerry (with irritation, as he picks it up, and places it again in
Sammy's hand). Try to keep a grip on it, man, 'n don't be
spillin' it all over the place. (*Sammy grips it like a sword.*)
Aw, not that way. Don't go to the opposite extreme. (*Arranging*
pen.) Nice 'n lightly between the finger 'n thumb. That way,
see? (*Speaking over to the Girl.*) He's not used to this kind of
thing, miss, but he'll be all right in a minute.

Sammy (standing still and looking vacantly at the wall).
Wanna poun' on demand.

Jerry (encouragingly). Go on, bend your back 'n write your
name. (*To the Woman who is writing her letter*) Mind movin'
over as far as you can, ma'am, to give him room to write his
name — he wants a pound on demand?

[*The Woman looks indignant, but moves a little away.*
Sammy bends down, gets the pen to the paper, slips and
slides along the ledge, nearly knocking the Woman down.

Jerry (in dismay). Aw, Sammy, eh, eh. Look at the form,
man. Can't you keep your balance for a second?

Woman (indignantly). This is a nice way to be scattered
about, writing an important letter to Tarraringapatam! (*To the*
Girl) Aren't you going to exercise a little control here, please?

Jerry (to the Woman). He's sawl right, he's sawl right,
ma'am.

Woman (*angrily*). No, it's not all right; it's anything but all right. (*Violently, to Sammy*) Remember you're in a Post Office, sir!

Sammy (*with drunken indignation*). Posht Offish! What's a Posht Offish? Haven't to take me shoes from off me feet in a Posht Offish, have I?

Jerry (*soothingly*). It's sawl right. No one wants you to take your shoes from off your feet. Here, lean on the ledge till I get a new form.

> [*He puts Sammy leaning against the ledge and goes over to get another form.*

Sammy (*meandering over to the Woman*). Shuh want me to take me shoes from offish me feet?

Jerry (*to the Girl*). Slip us another form, missie.

Sammy (*close to the Woman — emphatically*). Shuh hear me talkin' to you? Shuh want me to take me shoish from off me feet?

Jerry (*impatiently to the Girl*). Give's the form, miss, before he begins to get lively.

Girl (*busy at work*). Oh, just a minute. I gave you one a moment ago.

Sammy (*close to the Woman*). You push off, ma'am, please; thish plaish is occupied. Have to write me namish; need spaish; wanna pound on demand. (*The Woman ignores him.*) Push off when you're warned, can't you? Thish plaish ish occupied.

Jerry (*speaking over to Sammy from the counter*). Eh, eh, Sammy, there, control yourself, man. (*To the Girl*) Hurry up miss. Steady, Sam!

Sammy (*more emphatically, as the Woman ignores him*). Shuh hear me talkin' to you? Told you I wanted spaish. Push off, now — this plaish is occupied.

Jerry (*over to Sammy, in a warning voice*). Sammy! Steady!

Woman (*indignantly to Sammy*). How dare you tell me to push off? I'll have you know this is a public office, and I am engaged in important business.

Sammy (*aggressively*). Shuh don't want a pound on de-manish, so push off before I call the polish.

Jerry (*facing towards the Girl*). Calm, Sammy, calm.

> [*Sammy pushes the Woman as she is writing her letter, but she indignantly pushes back, and he finds it hard to keep his feet. He recovers and returns to the charge, pushes her again, but she pushes him more violently than before, sending him more than half-way towards the door; by a great effort he recovers and staggers back to the Woman with a look of determination on his face.*

Jerry (*to the Girl, as Sammy is staggering about — which Jerry does not see*). For God's sake, give's a form, missie.

Sammy (*pushing the Woman*). I have you taped, me lassie; wanta wash what're we doin': I have you taped, but I'll block you, me lassie!

> [*He pushes the Woman, who pushes him back; he tries to recover, but she follows him up, and pushes again so that Sammy staggers to the door, hits it, the door opens, Sammy staggers out into the street, and the door closes again. The Woman goes back to the writing of her letter.*

Jerry (*who is ignorant of Sammy's disappearance, rapping impatiently on the counter*). Eh, miss, missie, the form, miss, eh, the form, missie.

Girl (*impatiently slapping down a form on the counter*). That's the last you'll get.

Jerry (*combatively*). Oh, don't get too cocky, miss, for, after all, you're only a servant to the public. (*Tapping his chest*) It's the like of me that pays your wages. You're just here to serve the interests of the public, so don't get too cocky.

Girl (*tartly*). I don't want any impertinence, please.

Jerry (*hotly*). You'll do what's here to do accordin' to regulations. I wonder what'd happen if I sent in a chit of a complaint to the Postmaster-General?

> [*He turns round to go over to the writing-ledge and finds that Sammy has disappeared.*

Jerry (*staring round in bewilderment*). Where's he gone? Eh, where did Sammy go? (*He runs over to the Woman.*) Why the hell didn't you keep an eye on him when you knew he had a few up?

> [*He rushes to the door, pushes it open and runs out.*

Woman (*to the Girl*). Nice pair of drunken scoundrels. What are the police doing?

> [*The door swings open and Jerry enters, dragging Sammy in after him.*

Jerry (*indignantly, to the Girl*). Eh, will you speak to that lady over there, 'n keep her from interferin' with people transactin' public business?

> [*He leads Sammy back to the writing-ledge, spreads the form on the ledge for him, and carefully places a pen in his hand.*

Sammy (*as he is being led over*). Have that lasshie taped; thash lasshie over there, have her taped, so I have.

Jerry (*placing the pen in Sammy's hand*). Get your mit goin', Sammy, get your mit goin'. (*Sammy does not stir.*) Aaw, get down to it, man.

Sammy. Can't bend.

Jerry. Why can't you bend?

Sammy. Can't bend, can't stand; wanna chair.

Jerry (*impatiently*). Hold on tight, then, while I get you one. Hold tight, now.

> [*Sammy grips the writing-ledge grimly, as he stares over at the Woman who is writing at the other end. Jerry runs to the counter, acting and speaking so impetuously that the Girl does what is asked of her before she realizes what is happening.*

Jerry (*rapidly to the Girl*). The stool, missie, a lend of the stool; he can write his name safer sittin'; quick, missie!

> [*The Girl hands over a high stool, Jerry runs over to Sammy with the stool, helps Sammy to sit on it, settles the form, and again puts the pen in his hand. Sammy protrudes his tongue, and seems to find his coat in the way.*

Jerry. Oul' coat in the way, eh? Take it off, then, so's it won't clog your movements; young lady won't mind.

> [*After a good deal of pulling, Sammy, with the help of Jerry, gets off his coat.*

Woman (*sarcastically, staring at the pair*). Why don't you pull down the blinds and keep the light from hurting his eyes?

> [*Sammy gives a violent movement of anger, sweeping pen, ink, and form to the ground. Holding precariously to the ledge, he tilts his seat, slides over towards the Woman, and brings his face as close to hers as possible.*

Sammy (*angrily to the Woman*). Thish ish a Post Offish, see? No one allowed interfere with men hash businish to do. Wasn't reared yesterday, 'n I have you taped, me lasshie!

Jerry (*indignantly, to the Woman*). Whyja go 'n cause a commotion just as the man was doin' nicely? You've no right to interfere with men transactin' public business. (*Over to the*

Girl) See that, miss, see the way she interfered the minute the man was just doin' nicely?

Girl (*calmly*). I didn't see the lady interfering in any way.

Jerry (*indignantly*). Well, if you hadda had your eyes open, you'd ha' seen it. There doesn't seem to be any proper control in the place at all.

[*While Jerry is speaking, the Girl goes to the telephone, dials a number and listens. Jerry helps Sammy back to his original position on the stool.*

Girl (*at the telephone*). Hello; Pimblico Post Office speaking; send down one of your little boys, will you? Yes, at once, please.

[*She replaces the receiver and stands watching the two men, glancing, now and again, at the door.*

Jerry (*when he has settled Sammy*). Now don't fall asundher any more, for God's sake. (*To the Woman*) 'N no more of your condescendin' remarks, please, see?

Woman (*vehemently*). One word more from either of you, 'n I'll go straight out 'n bring in a policeman!

[*There are a few moments dead silence.*

Sammy (*breaking out excitedly*). Ja hear what she said? Ja hear? Bring a policeman in. That's what we get for trustin' people. What do I care for the poleish? Speak up, Jerry, 'n be a man — do I or do I not care for the poleish?

Jerry (*soothingly*). No, never; everyone who knows Sammy, knows that.

Sammy. Not if they were round me in dozens — do I or do I not?

Jerry. Not a word, Sammy, not a word; we rest silent about them things.

Sammy. Not a word. We don't rush round tellin' things; but we know, don't we, Jerry?

Jerry. Not a word. Don't let your nerves get jangled now. Slip your name down.

Sammy. Not another word. Poleeish! Do I or do I not care for the poleeish — you know, Jerry?

Jerry. Not a word — go on, get your name down.

Sammy (excitedly). Let her send for the poleeish! Wouldn't be long till they didn't know what was happenin'. Poleeish to the right of me, 'n to the left of me, 'n nothing left of them in the end but silver buttons for souvenirs!

Jerry. Rags, bones, 'n buttons, wha'? Go on — slip your name down.

[*The door opens and a huge Policeman enters. He walks slowly in, goes over to the counter, looks at the Girl, who points to the two men; the Policeman nods knowingly.*

Sammy (leaning over towards the Woman). We often plastered the roads with policemen, 'n left them thryin' out how they were going to get themselves together again!

Woman (scornfully). Oh, you did, didja?

Sammy (mockingly, to the Woman). Yes, we did, didn' we; we did did did didja, didn' we!

Policeman (coming over and standing near the two men). Now, then, do what you have to do, 'n go about your business.

[*The two men look round and see the Policeman. They stare at him for a few moments, and then turn their faces away, fixing their attention on the form. There is dead silence for a time, for the near presence of a Policeman is a great discomfort and very disconcerting.*

Jerry (almost in a whisper). Just there on the line, Sammy. Samuel, first name, see? Lead off with a big ess. A big ess, man, a big ess. Shape it into a big ess — capital ess — don't you know what a capital ess is? Here, I'll show you — give us a hold of the pen for a minute.

> [*Jerry takes the pen from Sammy and makes the necessary correction, and returns the pen to Sammy.*

Jerry. There y'are now. No, on ahead, cautious: a, m, u — I think — yes, u, double e, l — no, one e 'n two double ells — good God, what am I sayin' — only one double ell, only one double ell, man! You're not listenin' to me, Sammy. There's nothin' to prevent you doin' it right, if you'll only listen. You've nearly a dozen of ells down. Show it to me for a second.

> [*He takes the pen and removes roughly the unnecessary letters.*

Jerry (*warningly*). Now the next name, Adams; 'n make the letthers a little smaller, or you'll be a mile away from the form before the last one comes in sight.

Sammy (*in a weary voice*). Aw, I've had enough.

Jerry. You're too far ahead to give up now, man. T'other name, now. A big A for a start. Not as big as an elephant, now — you know what an ordinary capital A is. Oh, why did you let your hand slip? It'll have to do now. (*Turning and winking at the Policeman*) He's got a few up, but he's sawl right. (*To Sammy*) Now a little d, 'n a little u, 'n a little — wait a minute — I'm gettin' a little confused — a little m, a little n, 'n a little ess — a little ess, man! Now, come on, 'n we'll give it to the young lady.

Woman (*mockingly, to Jerry*). The poor man'll need a long rest, now.

> [*Jerry helps Sammy off the stool, and links him over to the counter, both of them trying to appear as if they were indifferent to the presence of the Policeman. He hands*

over the form to the Girl, who examines it, and looks at the name in the bank-book.

Jerry (humming, and trying to look unconcerned). Rum tum tiddley um tum, parley voo; rum tum tiddley um tum, parley voo; rum tum——

Girl (interrupting Jerry's humming). Couldn't give you a pound on demand with this signature. The signature on the form doesn't correspond with the signature in the bank-book in any way.

Jerry. It's his writin', isn't it, miss? An' both of the names is Adamsususes, aren't they?

Girl. They don't correspond. Sorry; but I can't let you have the money. I don't even know that the gentleman is really Mr. Adams.

Jerry (wild). Didja ever hear such consequential nonsense! *(To Sammy)* She says you're not Mr. Adams. *(To the Girl)* Of course he's Mr. Adams. Who else could he be, only Mr. Adams? Isn't he known all over the district where he lives, woman?

Girl. Why, then, didn't he go to the Post Office in his own district?

Jerry (impatiently). Because it's too busy an office, 'n we decided to come to a place where he could do what he wanted to do in comfort, 'n fill in his name at his ease.

Girl (with decision). I'm sorry; but I can't let the gentleman have the money.

Jerry (horrified). 'N what's he goin' to do, then?

Girl. Better call back again to-morrow, or the next day.

Jerry. He wants the money now, girl.

Girl. I can't give it to him.

Jerry (*to Sammy*). She says she won't give you the pound on demand.

Sammy. Wanna pound on demand.

Jerry (*to the Girl*). Hear what the depositor says? He's gotta get it.

Sammy. I've gotta get it.

Jerry (*to Sammy*). Of course you have. After the agony of gettin' things ship-shape, we're not goin' to stand any denial of our rights.

Policeman (*coming near*). Hasn't the young lady said she can't give it to you? So go on home, now, like decent men, an' forget all about it.

Jerry (*to the Policeman*). The man has gotta get his money, hasn't he?

Sammy (*dreamily*). 'Course I've gotta get it.

Policeman (*importantly*). Since he hasn't complied with the necessary preliminaries, he isn't entitled to withdraw his pound.

Jerry (*indignantly*). The only preliminary was the signin' of his name, wasn't it? 'N he signed his name, didn't he? Y'awl seen him signin' his name, didn't you? (*A pause*). Are yous all afraid to speak — did yous, or didn't yous?

Policeman. G'on now, g'on. (*To Jerry*) Y'ought to see that your comrade's incapable of discretion in withdrawin' anything from a Government corporation. G'on, now, like decent men.

Jerry (*appealingly*). He wants that pound special, I'm tellin' you. (*To Sammy*) Don't you, Sammy?

Sammy (*dreamily*). I gotta get it.

Jerry (*to the Policeman*). Hear that? Mind you, it's a serious thing to keep a man from gettin' his private property.

Policeman (*a little angry*). Here, g'on the pair of yous, before I lose me temper! You've been shown every leniency; so go home, now, like sensible, decent men, before I lose me temper.

Jerry. Give us back the bank-book, then.

Girl. Mr. Adams might lose it — I'll post it on to him to-morrow.

Jerry (*frightened*). He doesn't want you to post it. He wants it now — don't you, Sammy?

Sammy (*wearily*). I've gotta get it.

Policeman (*peremptorily*). Now go on home, like decent men, before I have to resort to exthremes. Go on 'n sleep over it, 'n to-morrow, after a wash 'n brush up, you'll be able to apply for your pound in an ordherly 'n sensible manner.

Jerry (*wildly*). 'N are we goin' to get nothin' out of all our efforts? Mind you, there'll be throuble about this.

Policeman (*roughly*). Ay, it'll start now if the two of yous don't bounce off 'n be well on your way home in a minute. (*He gently pushes them towards the door.*) G'on, now, you know your way.

Jerry (*scornfully*). 'N we thravelled miles to find this quiet place, so that he could sign his name in peace.

Woman (*mockingly, as they go out*). Isn't it a pity to disappoint the poor little children!

Sammy (*as they go out*). I've gotta get it.

> [*They go slowly and sorrowfully out. The Policeman holds the door open for them, and closes it when they have gone. The Woman goes over to the counter with her letter.*

Woman. Registered, please.

> [*The Girl takes the letter, registers it, and hands receipt to the Woman, who puts it in her bag and goes out.*

Girl (*to the Policeman*). Glad you hunted that pair of money philanderers out of the place.

Policeman (*taking her hand into his as he reclines over the counter*). You're lookin' fit 'n fair 'n sweet 'n rosy to-day, so you are.

Girl (*coyly*). Am I?

Policeman (*shyly*). Yes, y'are, so y'are.

> [*The door opens a little way then closes again. The Policeman lets go the Girl's hand and stands stiff, while the Girl pretends to be busy with a document.*

Girl. Thought that was someone.

Policeman. Same here. (*He takes her hand again.*) Y'are, really, lookin' fit 'n fair 'n sweet 'n rosy to-day, so y'are.

Girl (*archly*). Am I?

> [*The door suddenly swings open again, and Sammy appears, with Jerry steadying him from behind. They stand in the doorway, keeping it from closing with their shoulders. The Policeman and the Girl move away from each other.*

Jerry (*encouragingly to Sammy*). Go on, give them your ultimatum: tell them straight that you're goin' to write to the Postmaster-General before you settle down for the night. Go on, now — give them your ultimatum!

> [*They both come in towards the centre of the office.*

Sammy (*pointing a finger towards the Girl and the Policeman, which shakes and wanders from the floor to the ceiling as he

points). I have yous taped, two of yous 'n Postmaster-zheneral!
Taped, well taped I have, Postmaster-zheneral!

Jerry (*trying to cover up Sammy's vagueness*). Mr. Adams,
the depositor, has made up his mind to send a bitther complaint to the Postmaster-General about the way he's been
shunted about by public servants durin' his application for a
pound on demand. (*To Sammy*) Haven't you, Mr. Adams?

Sammy. I'm tellin' them, once for all, I've gotta get it.

Jerry. There y'are, you see; can't say I didn't warn you.
Somebody will be made to sit up for this.

Policeman (*loudly and ominously*). If the pair of yous aren't
gone for good in two ticks of the clock, yous'll spend the night
in a place that'll give the two of you plenty of time to complain
to the Postmaster-General. (*He makes a move towards them.*)
Be off, I'm tellin' yous, yourselves an' your pound on demand!

[*The two men are frightened by his move towards them, and
Jerry manœuvres Sammy swiftly to the door, and both
of them leave as quick as Sammy can travel.*

Jerry (*as they reach the door*). Somebody'll be made to sit
up for this, I'm tellin' you!

[*As the doors swing shut, they open again partly to show
Jerry's face glaring savagely into the office.*

Jerry (*shouting in from the partly opened door*). That's the last
penny of our money the Government'll ever get from us!

[*His face disappears, the door swings shut, and the curtain
comes down.*

HALL OF HEALING
A Sincerious Farce in One Scene

CHARACTERS IN THE PLAY

ALLELUIA (ALOYSIUS), *the Caretaker of the Dispensary*
THE OLD WOMAN
THE YOUNG WOMAN
BLACK MUFFLER   } *patients attending the Dispensary*
GREEN MUFFLER
JENTREE
A LAD
THE DOCTOR, *the Dispensary's Medical Officer*
THE APOTHECARY, *the Dispensary's Dispenser*
RED MUFFLER
GREY SHAWL, *Red Muffler's wife*

———

SCENE

The waiting-room of the Dublin Parish Dispensary for the Poor.
It is a winter's day.

The waiting-room of the Parish Dispensary in Dublin, on a winter's day. It is a place where the poor, sick, or diseased are looked at and, usually, rewarded with a bottle. It is an ugly room, drab, and not too clean. The few bright spots in it are the posters warning of disease. Running along the back wall is a bench on which the patients sit while waiting to go in to the Doctor. A shorter bench runs along the wall to the left. Beyond this bench is the entrance door which leads from the waiting-room to the hall, and thence into the street. In the centre of the back wall is a window which looks out into the street. Just to the right of this window, a wooden partition comes down, somewhat diagonally, through nearly two-thirds of the room, and then turns to the right, till it is joined to the side wall on the right. Within this partitioned part of the room are the Surgery and the Dispensary. A door in this partition wall, up towards the back, admits one to the Surgery. Another door in that part of the partition which has turned to the right, near the right side wall, gives entry to the Dispensary. To the left of this door is a small window (shuttered for the moment), with a narrow ledge in front of it, through which the remedies are handed out to the patients. On the Surgery door is the word DOCTOR *in black letters, and on the door of the Dispensary, the word* DISPENSER *also in black. On the back wall, to the left of the window, is a poster on which are the words in black print,* DIPHTHERIA: BEWARE! *Above the Dispensary window is another one on which are the words in red,* TUBERCULOSIS: BEWARE! *The Caretaker, Aloysius, nicknamed Alleluia, is fixing a third one, to the right of the window at back, on which are the words in green,* CANCER: BEWARE! *Through the window at back, it can be seen that the weather is bad; hurrying flakes of snow are falling in a zigzag way because of the cold wind blowing. At times through the scene, quick and thick flurries of snow pass by the windows outside.*

The patients are all of one patch, immersed in the same uncertainty and want. The lines of care and weariness on their countenances are the same, save that there are more on the face of the old than on the face of the young. The complexion of the younger is starkly pale; that of Jentree a lemon-yellow; that of the Old Woman, a yellowish-brown; that of Alleluia is pale, with a dot of yellow on the points of the cheeks; that of the Doctor a purplish-white; of the Apothecary a pale one, with a bare hint of struggling ruddiness through the paleness. Though differing in cast of countenance, shape and colour of clothing, they all carry in their faces the lines of conscious, or semi-conscious, uncertainty and resignation.

The face of Aloysius is a rather foolish one; his head is narrow at the top, developing down and out to form a square for a chin. His grey eyebrows gather into turned-up tufts at the corners; his tough nose tilts; and, though he has no moustache, a grey spade beard grows naturally, or has been trained, into a tilting tuft too. His mouth is wide, inclined to grin, and is always slightly agape. Whenever he moves across the room, he does so in a movement, half run, half glide, as if he skated on a surface fit only to glide over in places. As he glides he bends his body over and forward, as a stiff-backed bird might do, holding out his arms from his body as he glides and runs along.

Next to the Doctor (to whom he is subservient and of whom he is very much afraid), he is Lord of the Dispensary, dictating to the out-patients, and making things uncomfortable for them; though they try to please him, and follow his humours as well as they can. He wears a uniform of dark blue, the frock-coat reaching to below his knees. It is ornamented with silver buttons. His trousers are a bit short, coming only to the tops of his boots. His head is covered with a blue-peaked cap, having a wide top, and a narrow strap running along the butt of the peak is fastened on either side by a small silver button. A fussy old fool. He takes off his coat to tackle the job of tacking up the poster. He takes up a hammer, spreads out the poster, and with some difficulty hammers in a tack in one corner. Fixing the opposite one, he drops the tack, and curses, immediately ejaculating, 'Mea culpa, mea culpa'. He fixes that corner, and, in driving the third tack home, he hits his thumb, exclaims with pain, flings down the hammer, and thrusts the injured thumb under his armpit, first giving vent to a yell of agony.

Alleluia (pacing about the room, and nursing the injured thumb). Ooh! Sacred Heart! Me thumb's desthroyed! May th' curse o'—— *(He checks the profanation by trying to sing in a woeful way)* She's me lady love, she is me baby love. Oooh! *(He again yells in agony, and bends double to squeeze the injured member tighter under his armpit.)* Curse o'—— *(He checks himself.)* Oh, Holy St. Harmoniumagnus, succour me! *(He sings woefully again)* I know she likes me, I know she likes me, Because she says so — St. Serenium, ayse th' pain; ayse it, ayse th' agony! Preserve me from pain! Today, tomorrow, an' forever afther! Right on th' tenderest part!

> [*He goes moaning into the Dispensary, and the clank of bottles is heard.*

> [*Presently, the door leading into the Dispensary waiting-room from the street is cautiously opened, and the shawled head of an Old Woman peers into the room. Then the door is slowly opened, and the Woman enters. Her back is bent. Her boots are broken, and the skirt she wears is old and tattered at the hem. Shawl, skirt, boots, and all, are mud-coloured. She shivers and shudders as she comes in, slowly rubbing her gnarled*

hands to promote circulation. She goes over to the bench, and sits down stiffly. She coughs, and then wipes her mouth with the corner of her shawl. The clanking of the bottles stops. She gives another asthmatic cough, and again wipes her mouth with the end of her shawl. The shutter of the Dispensary window is pushed up, and Alleluia's head is thrust out; it looks round the room, and spies the Old Woman sitting on the bench. The head is withdrawn, the shutter pulled down, and Alleluia comes out of the Dispensary, wearing a bandage round the stricken thumb. He goes over with a glide to the Woman, catches her by the arm, pulls her from the seat, and guides her to the door.

Old Woman (*protesting feebly, but submitting calmly to ejection as one to whom it is a familiar part of life*). Ah, now, Mr. Aloysius, it's only a bare few minutes from the time of openin'. 'Clare to God, Alleluia, th' weather outside ud perish a body; an' I have within me oul' body a whole kingdom of aches an' pains!

[*Without a word Alleluia opens room door and leads her out, a look of determined indignation on his face; they can be heard going down the hall. Shortly after, he returns, and shuts the door. He cautiously completes the hanging up of the poster on the wall. He puts on his coat. Then he hurries into the Dispensary, comes out again with a sweeping-brush, and slides it over the floor, pushing whatever may be before it under the bench. While he sweeps, he sings softly, in the rather cracked voice of an old man, the chorus of 'The Rose of Tralee', pausing sometimes, as he pushes the brush, to do a bit of a waltz with it, and picking the song up again from where he left off, when its resumption seems convenient.*

Alleluia (singing):

    She was lovellee an' fayer as ay . . . rosebud of summer;

    But it wasn't her beautay aylone . . . that . . . won me;

    Aah, no; 'twas they truth in her . . . eyes . . . ever beamin',

    That med me lovev Mary . . . they rose of . . . Thraa . . . lee!

> [*Nearing the end of the chorus, he is near the door of the Dispensary, and, doing a kind of dancing swirl right around, as he sings the last line, he glides into the Dispensary and closes the door behind him.*

> [*After a moment or two, the entrance door opens and Red Muffler, a young man of twenty-five, enters the room. He looks thin and a little careworn. He is very poorly and thinly dressed; his muddy-black trousers are patched with black cloth on one knee. His neck is protected by a thin, red woollen muffler, and a dark tweed cap, dotted with snowflakes, is pulled low down over his eyes. He looks poor, cold, and miserable; but there seems to be some element of grit in his standing. He takes his cap off, and, holding it by the peak, whirls it round to shake the heavier dampness from it; then he replaces it on his head. Between each forefinger and thumb, he pinches together each leg of his trousers, and flicks them in an effort to make them feel drier. The Old Woman's head appears round the edge of the door, peering nervously into the room. Red Muffler sees her.*

Red Muffler (to Old Woman). Come in, old lady; here is more sheltthered than th' hall, an' a heaven from th' sthreet.

Old Woman (deprecatingly). I'll do lovely here. If himself seen me, it's out into th' sthreet I'd go again, an' a body pushin' hard to eighty years isn't proof against th' chill o' th' sleet, an' th' chatther of th' interferin' wind outside.

Red Muffler (*irritated by her timidity*). Aw, come in, woman, for God's sake! It's this fear of offendin' that keeps us all so far from th' spice of comfort.

Old Woman (*timidly crossing the threshold*). I wondher if I ought to venthure it? Alleluia 'ill only be shovin' me out again. (*She crosses herself.*) He's a good Catholic, an' maybe he won't now.

Red Muffler (*decisively*). Aw, go and sit down, woman. I'll know how to deal with this Alleluia of yours when he shows himself.

Old Woman (*wandering over to the bench*). Th' docthor before this one gave us a bad habit, always leavin' ordhers to let us in before openin' time, if th' weather was grim, or rain was fallin', or even when the sun happened to be too boistherous.

Red Muffler. An' what's wrong with th' present docthor?

Old Woman. Aw, he's one o' th' surly specimens. (*She rises stiffly, bending double, and groaning, to come close to him.*) He's partial to th' dhrop. He has th' life frightened outa poor oul' Alleluia. (*She whispers*) He can't abide you to come on Mondays, because of his feelin' frightful afther Sunday's rest.

Red Muffler. Why do you come on Monday, then?

Old Woman. It's me one free day. I have to work on all the others.

Red Muffler. Is he doin' yeh anny good?

Old Woman. Aw, divil a good, so far; but I'm always hopeful he may.

Red Muffler. An' is he hopeful?

Old Woman. Divil a hopeful. He just says I'm wastin' his time comin' here; that me back'll never straighten, an' th' ache'll never end. But you can never tell with God.

Red Muffler (clapping his cold hands against his sides). An' how much d'ye make outa your work?

Old Woman. A shillin' a day, son; five shillin's a week.

Red Muffler. Jasus, that's not much!

Old Woman. It's something, son. You see, I can do only rough an' heavy work now. Me oul' hands is too shaky for any fancy job. I don't need much. I won't worry if only I can out-last life workin'. *(Anxiously)* D'ye know, I don't really think I ought to stay here — a few more slaps from the flauntin' wind, an' one more scattherin' of rain over me can't do me much harm.

Red Muffler (ignoring her anxiety). An' have you no-one to fight for you; no childhren to stand up for you?

Old Woman. Fight, is it? Fightin' only makes things worse. Of course, I've children, but all married, an' hard set them-selves to live. There's one blessin' — I can offer everything up to God.

Red Muffler (venomously). Misery isn't much of a gift to give to God, is it?

Old Woman (shocked and staring — after a pause). Ah, son, don't say a thing like that! We're too poor to take th' risk of sayin' serious things. We're told God is good, an' we need every little help we can get.

Red Muffler. An' th' kind docthor before this fellow come — where did he go?

Old Woman. Aw, he went into his grave. Cancer, I'm told. With th' aid o' dhrugs, he kept himself goin' for a year an' a day; then, he was silently seen no more.

Red Muffler (*echoing her*). Silently seen no more! Will this damned doctor never come! Such as us 'have barely time to glimpse a gleam that's kind before it hurries to the dark again. It's afther ten, and that damned docthor isn't here!

Old Woman (*anxiously*). Why, aren't you feelin' well, son?

Red Muffler. Me? Oh, I'm all right. It's our little girl o' nine: our first one. She's been bad a week; she's worse; now, we're afraid she'll soon be something silently seen no more. (*Tensely*) The child is bad; th' child is worse; th' child is chokin'. (*Agonisingly*) Jesus Christ, ha' mercy!

Old Woman (*soothingly*). I wouldn't be fancyin' death for your little one, son. She'll be all right. God is good. They tell us that God's thought is roomy with anxiety for the very young.

Red Muffler (*impatiently*). I know what they tell us, I know, woman; but it's past ten; an' ten's th' hour, an' th' blighter should be here. (*The organ is heard playing.*) What music is that?

Old Woman. An organ in the church next door; every Monday someone plays it: practisin', maybe. When th' wind's this way, you can hear it. The caretaker here dances like a fool, and chants an Alleluia ditty whenever it sounds. That's why we call him Alleluia. (*She comes nearer.*) An oul' fool!

Red Muffler. Me feet's numb. It's not good to be left standin' here in these wet things. I'm seepin'.

Old Woman. When you're my age, son, you'll be well used to them things.

> [*He stamps his feet heavily on the floor in an effort to give them the feel of life. The shutter on window in Dispensary is suddenly pulled up, and the head of Alleluia, cap and all, is thrust through it. The head peers around*

to see who has made the noise, sees Red Muffler, and the
head is pulled in again, while the shutter is pulled down
with a snap. Then the door of the Dispensary is opened,
and Alleluia slides out and over to the Red Muffler. He
takes him by the arm and tries to guide him to the
entrance door, but he is resisted, and Red Muffler doesn't
budge.

Red Muffler (shaking off Alleluia's hold). Here, you — what's
bitin' you?

Alleluia (a little taken aback by the unexpected resistance). You
can't stay here. No one's to cross the sthreet door till th'
regulation time o' openin'. (*He snatches Red Muffler by the arm
again.*) Come on, now — out!

Red Muffler (violently shaking off Alleluia's hold). G'way,
you fussy, fiddlin' fool!

[*A little frightened, and deciding that discretion is needed,*
Alleluia side-steps from Red Muffler, spots the Old
Woman — now cowering in a corner — and glides over
swiftly to where she sits. He catches her arm; she
obediently rises, and he begins to guide her over to the
entrance.

Old Woman (timidly apologetic). I musta strayed in be
mistake, Mister Alleluia — I mean, Mr. Aloysius. Th' sleet
an' the bullyin' wind has made th' sthreet unkind, sir. Yes,
th' wind must ha' blew me in, mister. Without me noticin'
either. You'll excuse me, sir; for I've many burdens of aches an'
pains to try to hide from th' blowin' blight of th' weather.

Alleluia (decisively). Yeh can't hide your aches an' pains here,
ma'am. You can't expect to have Alleluia hours of comfort at
your time o' life, or in your circumstances. Th' last docthor
near ruined yous all, so he did, with his scorn of regulations;
with his 'make the bareness brighter', an' his 'th' most o'

them won't last a lot longer'. Had he lived, he'd ha' wanted cushions for your poor backsides. Th' waste of it! I'd like to know how we'd fare without th' regulations.

Old Woman (meditatively). Th' last one always had a winsome word for th' sick an' dyin', so he had.

Alleluia. Because he was sick an' dyin' himself — that's why. Out you go, an' don't put your nose in again, till th' docthor arrives.

Old Woman (half turning to glance at Red Muffler). Th' gentleman behind us, sir, advised me to shelther in outa th' weather.

Alleluia (pushing her out by the door). Out you go!

[*During all this Red Muffler has taken no notice, making no effort to defend the Old Woman; but has turned his back on the other two, and is now staring hard at one of the posters.*

Old Woman (reaching the door, hesitates, turns suddenly round, and runs across the room till she is half-way to where Red Muffler is standing — bitterly). You went before me when I was comin' in, but you're not before me goin' out! You keep your courage secret, you do. (*She makes the motion and the sound of spitting scornfully towards him*) That's your value to this poor oul' woman, you poor morsel of a man! (*Alleluia has now got behind her with a movement that is half a run, half a glide, and hastens to shoo her out as a drover might a cow, adding an occasional shove with his hand to her back. As she nears the entrance door — fervently*) Thanks be to God who spared th' last poor docthor be givin' him death, an' deliverin' him from th' lousy lot of us!

[*She disappears out by the door, Alleluia following close on her heels. Red Muffler turns slowly away from the poster, and sinks down to sit on the bench, resting with his elbow on knee, his head on his hand. After a pause, the Doctor whirls into the room, fussier even than old Alleluia, followed meekly by the Caretaker. The Doctor is of middle height, rather plump, and widening perceptibly around the belly. His face — half concealed now by a thick white wool muffler — is turning to a purplish tinge by hard drinking. His eyes are small and hard, his eyebrows thick and shaggy. Had he his black bowler hat off, it could be seen that he is bald, save for a few reddish-grey hairs brushed over the crown, in an effort, maybe, to hide a big expanse of polished skull. He is wearing a heavy brown topcoat; and his lower legs are encased in shining black leather leggings; a serviceable umbrella is in his left hand, a satchel in his right one. As he enters, he gives a sudden belch, and he ejaculates, as if to himself, but quite audibly: 'Jasus!' He catches sight of Red Muffler, and turns to Alleluia.*

Doctor. Who's that fella? What's that fella doin'?

Alleluia. He's waitin' for you, sir.

Doctor. An' how'd he get in before the regulation time?

Alleluia. He just came in without by your leave from a soul. I expostulated with him, but he wouldn't budge for no-one. Wouldn't budge an inch.

Doctor. Then th' street door must have been open to let him in.

Alleluia (sliding to the left and to the right of the Doctor, and back again). I left it open, sir, for a spessesscific purpose.

Doctor. For a what? What d'ye mean, man?

Alleluia (again sliding to right and left, and around, the Doctor so that the Doctor has to turn to follow what he's saying). For you, sir; I didn't want you to be fouled with the weather an' you fussin' with th' key for th' keyhole.

Doctor (impatiently). Stop that buzzing round me; you make me giddy, man. I'm quite competent to find the key-hole without a fuss. Don't leave that door open again till the regulation time. If I've forgotten the key, I can ring, can't I? *(As Alleluia is silent)* Damn it, I can ring, can't I?

Alleluia. Yis, yis; of course you can ring; 'course you can, sir.

Doctor. And you're not deaf, man, as well as bothered, are you?

Alleluia. Me deaf? *(With a dancing glide before the Doctor)* I'd hear the cuckoo before it came, sir.

Doctor. Well, hear the surgery bell when it rings, for I'm not in a waiting mood today. How many are outside, d'ye know?

Alleluia. I seen six or seven or eight, or maybe nine, when I peeped into the street.

Doctor (sarcastically). Are you sure it wasn't ten, now?

Alleluia. It might ha' well been ten, for the sleet was fallin' between me an' them. More than ten, maybe, sir.

Doctor. Well, you can get them in, and, mind you, no delay when the bell rings. Immediately one enthers, pop another at the edge of the surgery door to be ready when the bell sounds again.

Alleluia (doing another gliding dance to the right, to the left of the Doctor). On their tiptoes; ears cocked; tense with listenin', prepared to spring forward when they hear a tinkle.

Doctor (thrusting the umbrella under his right arm, and gripping the shoulder of Alleluia with his left hand, which he uses to give him a shake). Keep still, you rubbered image of desolation! When the bell gives two quick rings, it's you I want, not a patient. And listen: no gossiping while you're on duty — d'ye hear?

Alleluia. Gossip, is it? Me gossip? An' on duty? Aw, never! Th' only words I ever uses is expended on expostulations. Never fear, sir; I keep well within th' silences of devotion. Gossip on duty is not good company.

Doctor (explosively). Aren't you always at it! Expostulations! Give your expostulations a rest today, and just shove them in to me.

Alleluia. You don't know them, doctor; if you did, you wouldn't wondher any. Not a one o' them'll budge without an expostulation.

Doctor (wildly). Looka here, if you don't learn to quit yourself better than you do, I'll complain to the Guardians, by God, I will! (*He gives a more violent and sickly belch.*) Ooh, damn it! You're making me worse! If you have me yelling at you today, it'll be th' worse for you. Have you th' Surgery fire going well?

Alleluia (cheerfully — and beginning to slide about again). Yissir; oh, ay: it's a beauty; all aglow, an' most enticin'. I'd hurry in to it, an' get them damp things off you.

Doctor. They're not damp! (*Near a shout*) I came in a cab!

Alleluia. An' a wise man you were, doctor, to do it.

Doctor (impatiently). Get them in, man, and get them out! No dallying today.

> [*He hurries towards the Surgery; Red Muffler rises again from the bench to meet him. Alleluia hurries out by the entrance door, and soon returns followed by the patients, sorry-looking men and women from the tenements. Alleluia stands at the entrance door ushering them in, and waving them to the benches. As they troop in, the organ is heard playing again, and the poor patients seem*

to fall in with the rhythm of the tune as they drag
themselves to the benches.

[Among them are Black Muffler; the old bent-back
woman; a Young Woman of twenty-three, who, behind
her hand, gives an occasional dry, hard cough; Mr.
Jentree, a man of forty-five, dressed in a mode of faded
respectability — bowler hat, black, somewhat dis-
coloured; faded brown tweed coat, waistcoat, and
trousers; stiff white collar and black tie; and a brown
mackintosh. As he enters, his head is shaking, a strained
look of anxiety disturbs his face which is fortified by a
short beard and moustache. He walks uncertainly with
the aid of a stick. He sits down between the Young
Woman and the Old Woman. While seated, first his
right leg, and then his left one, gives a sudden and
spasmodic jerk, signifying a nervous disorder. Among
them is Green Muffler, a man of about thirty-five, clad
in the rough clothes of a labourer — corduroy trousers,
old khaki coat from the remains of the first world war,
thick coat of a faded dark blue, and a green muffler
round his neck. When he enters, he looks nervously
around him, as if asking himself if it were well for him
to be there. And when he sits down on the last bit of
bench, he stretches his head forward to look at the
posters. The other patients are but variants of the others
in feature and colour of clothing.

Red Muffler (going in front of the Doctor before he gets to the
Surgery door). Excuse me, sir; I want to ask you about our
kid.

Doctor (brusquely). What kid? Sit down, sit down, man, and
take your turn.

Red Muffler. I'm not ill meself, sir; I've only come about our little girl who's very bad.

Doctor (impatiently). Sit down, sit down, till I'm ready for you.

Red Muffler (speaking rapidly for fear the Doctor would get away). You seen her a week ago, sir. She's worse, an' th' missus's afraid for her.

Doctor (sharply and rapidly). Oh, sit down when you're told, man!

Red Muffler (submissively complying). Yessir.

[*The Doctor hurries into the Surgery. Alleluia obsequiously closes door after him. Red Muffler resumes his seat nervously, pulling his coat round him; buttoning it up, and then opening it again.*

Young Woman (coughing behind her hand). He's in a bad mood today.

Old Woman. When's he any other way? Since the last doctor's death th' last light left us has gone out.

Black Muffler (morosely). What odds? Th' fella taken away done no more for us than this fella that's left. It's a new doctor, but it's th' old, old treatment. I dunno that th' last one was fit to be a docthor at all.

Old Woman (scornfully). You dunno! Who're you to dunno? Why wasn't he fit?

Black Muffler. Well, ma'am, th' last time he saw me, he said what I needed was betther food, a finer house to live in, an' a lot more enjoyment. An' when I said couldn't you give me a bottle, docthor, he laughed at me, so that I felt ashamed of me life. An' afther what he had said, d'ye know what he said then?

Jentree (impatiently). Then what did he say, what did he say, then?

Black Muffler. My good young man, he said, you can't expect to dhrink health into you out of a bottle. Nobody knows how frightened I felt!

Young Woman. Wouldn't any sensible one be frightened at th' edge on a remark like that!

Old Woman. Poor innocent man — no wondher th' good God took him to Himself!

Black Muffler. When he saw th' fright I was in, he put a hand on me shouldher, and said, Looka, says he, if health could be got out of a bottle, says he, I'd be th' healthiest man alive. An' me heart galloped into th' fear that th' poor man wasn't a docthor at all! Unless he was beginnin' to go out of his mind. I've never been th' same since.

Jentree. I dunno how life could be lived without some kinda bottles.

Old Woman. What if th' poor man did make a slip aself — it's a wise man doesn't. He just had some kind of a kink against bottles.

> [*Meanwhile, Alleluia has gone into the Dispensary, and returns with a stick of chalk. With this he draws a straight line on the floor, half-way between the bench and the Surgery door. Just outside this door, draws a circle. Within the circle, he puts a patient facing the door, and places another patient toeing the line, facing, too, towards the Surgery door. The Surgery bell rings. Alleluia hurries the patient in the circle into the Surgery, shoves the other patient into it, while another one toes the line. When the first patient comes out, she goes to the Dispensary, hands in a bottle, gets it back full, and then*

she goes away by the entrance door, shivering with an-
ticipation at what she will meet outside. This goes on
rapidly till a stream of patients have passed in, come out,
and gone away. Alleluia hurries each in when the bell
tinkles, hurries each to the Dispensary window for the
medicine, and then hurries each out of the place. This is
the common measure of the place, and it goes on rapidly
till Black Muffler passes from the line to the circle, and
from the circle into the Surgery. As each poor patient
comes out to go away, Alleluia waylays him or her, hold-
ing a card out to them, and asking a penny for the Holy
Souls, that Masses may be said for their redemption
from Purgatory. When he gets a penny, he pricks a
space in the card he holds in his hand with a pin. The
organ is heard playing the same tune during the pro-
cession of patients, and Alleluia goes about in a dancing
slide   to   the   tune,   chanting,   mockingly,   'Alleluia,
Alleluia, Alleluia', waylaying the patients for pennies
at intervals, challenging them with the phrase 'Remem-
ber the Holy Souls in Purgatory'. Black Muffler comes
out of the Surgery cautiously and softly shuts the door
behind him.

Black Muffler (*gesturing back towards the Surgery with his*
thumb — in a whisper). Hunted me out! Lyin' down on a
couch, with th' Dispenser givin' him a cordial. Looks like a
cut-down daisy. We'll be here all day.

Young Woman. Maybe it'll give time for the weather to clear.

[*Alleluia glides down the room, bends down, hands on*
knees, before Green Muffler, and stares at him. The
patients watch the glide, and Black Muffler — again in
the circle — and the rest — except Jentree — turn to
watch and listen.

Alleluia (to Green Muffler). You're a new customer here, aren't you?

Green Muffler (staring back at him). I was never here before, if that's what you mean.

Alleluia. An' what are you complainin' of, me man?

Green Muffler. Eh? (*Stretching out his right arm carefully and slowly*) Oh, just this arm o' mine — it hurts terrible when I thry to do anything serious.

Alleluia. Aah, rheumatism!

Green Muffler (shortly). Naw, it's not rheumatism! I know what rheumatism is.

Alleluia (thoughtfully). It might be something goin' against th' blood strame.

Green Muffler (with sharpness and mockery). Are you th' docthor, or wha'?

Alleluia (importantly). I'm next to th' docthor. Where's your bottles?

Green Muffler (somewhat startled). Bottles? What bottles?

Alleluia. There's no use o' you comin' here if you're not thoughtfully and thoroughly supplied with bottles. Every commencer must have three — one for a draught, one for a liniment, and one for a mixture. You can't go into the doctor's presence unless you are in possession of three comely and commodious bottles.

Green Muffler (impressed). I didn't know nothin' about bottles.

Old Woman (leaning forward as far as she can from the bench towards Green Muffler). You might need only one, son; but th' nature of your particular throuble might require two; an' in a diversified complaint, three bottles might be called for;

so you have to be prepared. Stands to reason, a patient must be provided with a bottle, or two, or three bottles. As likely as not, son, you'll be a three-bottle man.

> [*The patients are now more interested than ever in the discussion; the one in the circle of chalk moves out of it to be nearer; and the one toeing the line moves nearer too. Jentree is the only one who is occupied with himself, and takes no notice.*

Alleluia (*not liking the interference — turning towards the Old Woman, with his body still bent double and hands on knees*). If you'll allow me, ma'am, I'd have you notice that this would-be patient is receivin' official attention an' insthruction respectin' any bottles necessary in combination with his ailment.

Young Woman (*coughing behind her hand*). One ud never know, be th' common look of them, that bottles was so important. With every patient, bottles there must be.

Black Muffler. Bottles there was, bottles there is, bottles there must be!

Alleluia (*angrily — to the patients in general*). Are yous goin' to have me expostulatin' all th' day! Close your gobs, an' cease from shattherin' me explanations to this man!

Green Muffler. Th' whole place seems to be seethin' with bottles. An' where am I goin' to get them?

> [*The Surgery bell has been signalling for Alleluia — by giving two quick, consecutive rings — several times; but all are so excited over, and interested in, the bottles that no-one takes the slightest notice.*

Old Woman (*over to Green Muffler*). If you've thruppence on you, son, you'll get them in some pub: black porther or green mineral bottles — it doesn't matther, for they're all good of their kind.

Alleluia (*accompanying Green Muffler out by the entrance*). An' remember, they must be all rinsed clean so as to be in a receptionable condition for th' contention of medicine.

> [*The bell sounds its two quick, consecutive rings again, this time with venomous clarity in the now silent room, startling the patients back into meek and anxious attention.*

Young Woman (*agitated*). Holy Saint Juniper o' Judea, there's th' docthor callin' a patient!

Old Woman (*to the patient who has been standing in the chalk circle — vigorously*). Off you go; in with you!

Black Muffler (*bewildered by the sudden change of topic*). Who? Is it me, is it?

Old Woman (*rapidly*). You, you; yes, you. Hop it, man!

Young Woman (*beginning before the Old Woman ends*). Quick. Yes, you!

Jentree (*beginning before the Young Woman ends*). Before he's out on top of us, roarin'!

> [*Black Muffler makes a bewildered rush for the Surgery door, which he opens. He goes in, but immediately comes out again, pushed back by the Doctor, who is angry and furious.*

Doctor (*wildly*). Not you, not you! Aloysius I rang for! Good God, that fellow'll drive me mad! (*Shouting*) Aloysius!

Alleluia (*sliding into the room again — full of hurry and fear*). Sir, sir; here, sir!

Doctor (*stormily*). Where were you, you dolt! Didn't you hear the bell? You'll quit this very week-end! What were you doing, you deaf oul' ditherer?

Alleluia (*rapidly*). Explainin' regulations to a patient, sir, about bottles.

Doctor (*furious*). You fool, what do bottles matter! My pen — where is it? Pen, pen, man!

Alleluia (*flustered, but smiling*). Pen? Oh, the pen, is it? Oh, yes, the pen. Let me think, now. I remember, yes; th' apothecary got a loan of it, sir.

Doctor (*angrily*). Get it back then, at once. He's no business to touch it! Let him get a pen of his own. This is th' third or fourth time he's pinched it!

Alleluia (*deprecatingly*). Not pinched, sir; oh, no, not pinched it.

Doctor (*roaring*). Pinched, I say! (*He gives a half-belch ending in a sigh — ejaculating as if to himself*) Oh, God! I'm in a shockin' state! (*To Alleluia — angrily*) Why th' hell d'ye let him take it?

Alleluia (*whisperingly*). Between ourselves, sir, I'm tired expostulatin' with him. You'd want to chain it to your desk, sir.

Doctor. Wish I could chain you where you'd be hidden from view! (*Pushing Alleluia from him*) Go, an' get th' pen! (*To Red Muffler, who has risen, and now takes a step towards him*) Oh, sit down, you; sit down!

> [*Crestfallen, Red Muffler does so.*
> [*The Apothecary's head is poked out of the Dispensary window; the head is completely bald, except for a tiny web of fringe above the forehead; a thick moustache covers the upper lip, and almost hides the mouth; it juts out aggressively at each side of the face. The head twists round in the direction of the voices.*

Apothecary's Head (*shouting*). Aloysius; eh, Aloysius!

Alleluia (*running round to the window*). Yessir.

Apothecary's Head (*thrusting out an arm holding a pen*). Here's th' damned pen for him!

[*Alleluia snatches the pen, and rushes back to the Doctor, who snatches it from him.*

Doctor (*indicating with his pen Black Muffler who had stood within the chalk circle*). You there — come in. Come on, come on!

[*He goes into the Surgery.*

Alleluia (*fussy as ever — getting behind the patient, and pushing him along*). Go on, go on, go on!

[*Green Muffler enters by the entrance door. He is damp and shivery. He carries a porter bottle under an arm, and the neck and shoulders of mineral-water bottles are sticking out from the side pockets of his coat. He sits down, silent and morose, on the end of the bench.*

[*Alleluia beckons the Young Woman, and places her within the chalk circle. He takes another patient from the bench and puts him toeing the line; bending down to shove back a foot that ventures over it, arranging the feet so that they exactly touch the sacred chalk line.*

Alleluia (*petulantly fixing the foot*). Keep the feet determined toein' the line exact, will you!

Young Woman (*nervously*). I hope I won't be called on to stand too long here — I always feel shaky when I stand for long in th' one place.

Old Woman. He'll take a long time between patients today; always does when he's bad from booze.

Jentree (*giving a sudden jerk in his seat*). You know, if I don't get some specific attention soon an' sudden, something terrible's bound to happen. I'll fall, paralysed, from me neck down!

Old Woman (soothingly). You're lettin' it, whatever it is, play on you too much, son.

Jentree (testily). Aw, for God's sake, woman, talk sense. Can't I feel me legs goin' dead? D'ye imagine I can go on not noticin' things? (*A leg gives a spasmodic jerk.*) Oh! Did yous all see that? (*To Alleluia*) Eh, misther, I'll have to be let in at oncst!

Alleluia (with a sweeping glide towards Jentree, and a bend-down to place his face in front of Jentree's). You'll wait till th' regulation tinkle of th' bell tells you to go.

Jentree (as the other leg gives a spasmodic jerk upwards). Oh! There, did yous all see that one go up? There's no deception, mind yous — I'm really in a desperate condition!

Young Woman (in the circle). Poor man! An' what gave you them terrible jerks? What did th' docthor say?

Jentree (with scorn). Th' docthors! Th' one before this one, an' this fella, too, said it was because of too much imbibin' of wine.

Old Woman (startled). Wine? An' where would you come across th' quantity of wine to give you them sharp an' sudden jitters?

Jentree. I was a wine porther, ma'am, but th' little I lowered through th' years couldn't possibly ha' done it.

Old Woman (realising the cause, but not willing to hurt). Looka that now. I wouldn't say all; but it might, it only might, mind you, have had a little to do with it.

Jentree (getting on to his feet with a shivering jerky movement). Oh! Th' bottle I get is doin' me damn all of good! An' th' wather I have to dhrink's makin' me worse! Looka, I'm thremblin' all over!

Old Woman (to the other patients who are now all interested in Jentree). His mind's sthrayin'. *(To Jentree)* Wather? What wather are you dhrinkin', son?

Jentree (venomously). Th' wather them getts o' docthors ordhered me to lower — more'n half a gallon a day. *(He sinks back on to the bench.)* Me left leg's lost its motion. Not in a year, mind you, but in a day! I'd like to see him thryin' it himself. *(He jerks up from the bench again.)* I'll have to be carried home, if this goes on! What manner o' mortal man could swally a tank of wather in a single day?

Old Woman. Indeed, son, th' boyo inside wouldn't like to have to do it himself.

Jentree. I feel close to death when I see the sight of it!

Old Woman. Th' sight of what, son?

Jentree (explosively). Wather, woman; th' wather!

Alleluia (coming close to the talkers). There's only one thing, ma'am, manifested enough to negify th' effects o' wine, an' that's wather; an' th' patient would be well advised to gulp it down, gulp it down with determination, ad lib.

Old Woman (eagerly — to Jentree). Hear that, son? Mr. Aloysius knows what's good for you! Wholesome stuff is wather. Gulp it down, son, an' it's bound to negify any wine that may be ripplin' round in you still: ad lib's th' only way!

Jentree (to Old Woman — determinedly). I'd have you remember, ma'am, that I'm th' custodian of me own ailments, an' am fully endorsed on their concern and their keepin'! *(Indignantly — to Alleluia)* Gulp it down! I wondher would you relish gulpin' cold wather down you till your heart was stunned into stoppin' its beatin'? Would you like to gulp cold wather down you till every vital organ in your poor body was frightened of what was floodin' into them? Negify th' effects o' wine! An' if I go on, what'll I take to negify th' effects of wather?

Old Woman (*to Jentree*). Sure that's the difficulty, son. (*To Alleluia*) If th' poor man has to negify th' wine with wather, and then has to negify the wather with wine, sure th' poor man'll burst himself thryin' to find a solution for his ailment.

Jentree (*to Old Woman*). Sure that's what I'm up against all the time, an' no-one'll listen to me! (*Rising shaking to his feet and sitting down again — a little hysterical*) What's keepin' that fella inside! I'm goin' fast. Th' thremors is mountin' me spine. I'll be gone in a minute, if he doesn't hurry to have a look at me!

Young Woman (*from the circle*). Poor man, y'are in a terrible state! Maybe you'd like to take my turn? I'm in no hurry, so I'm not. Indeed, I'd rather wait as long as I can in th' hope th' weather ud be betther when I set out for home.

Old Woman (*to Jentree — encouragingly*). Yes, do; go on, son; take your chance of an earlier overhaul.

[*She rises, and, with the help of the Young Woman — coughing with the exertion — planks Jentree in the circle. He is shaky, nervous, and leans heavily on his stick. The Young and the Old Women then return, and sit down on the bench. The Surgery door opens gently, and Black Muffler enters the waiting-room on tiptoe, a frightened look on his face. He closes the Surgery door softly, and gives an admonitory and warning gesture with a prescription he is holding in a hand.*

Black Muffler (*with a significant wave of a hand*). Husssh! He's in a murtherin' mood today! Can't sit aysy a second. Went out once, an' I heard him thryin' to retch. He'll take ages to get through today. Jasus, we poor have a lot to bear!

Red Muffler (*rising to his feet — angry and fierce*). An' why do they bear it! Even with the best docthor in its bosom, what kind of a kip is this place? I deny that this is all that God has got to give us! Even with the best music of a church organ, what betther could we do here but dance a dance of death! I won't do it; I won't do it! By God, if that fella inside refuses to come to our sick kid, I'll know th' reason why!

> [*He sinks down on the bench again, wiping his forehead with a soiled rag he has taken from a pocket. After this outburst, for a little while, there is a dead silence, the patients, standing and sitting, staring at the fiercely-spoken Red Muffler.*
>
> [*Then Black Muffler goes to the window of the Dispensary, hands in his prescription and a bottle; waits a moment, then gets the bottle back filled with a rich yellow fluid. He comes to the middle of the room, and holds the bottle from him towards the light.*

Black Muffler (*holding the bottle at arm's length*). Oh, a lovely yella, this time; th' last was blue.

Young Woman. Mine was red, so it was.

Old Woman. Show us. (*He hands her the bottle, and she holds it out at arm's length.*) So 'tis — a gorgeous yella! (*She hands the bottle back to him.*) Be th' look of it, son, that should do you a power o' good. This fella thinks more o' bottles than th' other fella did — I'll say that of him!

Alleluia (*down at the entrance, beckoning Black Muffler to go*). Eh, you, with the black muffler, there; you've been fully medicamented, an' you've been handed your documented mixture; (*he glides up to Black Muffler*) so no more chit-chat, but go; but before you go, remember the Holy Souls.

Black Muffler (*ignoring Alleluia's appeal — pocketing the bottle*). I'll enther a new lease o' life when I stoke meself up with this documented stimulant, wha'? I'll renew th' bottle, he says. Well, we'll thry it once more, anyway.

> [*Alleluia slides and glides up to Black Muffler, catches him by the arm, and glides down with him to the entrance door, ushering him out to the street.*

Jentree (becoming more nervous). What's keepin' him; what's th' fella doin' at all? I'm gettin' worse. I'll be down prostrate, numb an' nameless, before th' fella lets me in!

Old Woman (encouragingly). Keep calm, son. Take your thoughts off yourself.

Jentree (turning angrily to Old Woman). Don't be rattlin' nonsense into me mind, woman, an' me in agony! I need immediate aid to countheract what's comin'. I can't wait. I want help at once; now! (*He totters rapidly over to the Surgery door; kicks it below with a foot, bangs it above with his stick.*) These docthors wouldn't blink an eyelid if a man passed into oblivion! (*He again kicks and hammers on the door.*) Eh, eh, you in there, does medical discretion always go disregarded in this place?

> [*As Jentree is hammering at the door, it suddenly opens, and the Doctor, furious with anger, appears. Jentree totters back a little, and the patients sit straight and still with respect and a little fear. The patient toeing the line runs off to sit down demurely on the bench.*

Doctor (in an agony of rage). What's this, my God, what's all this? (*To Jentree*) Was it you who hammered at the door?

Jentree (smilingly). Me, sir? I just gave a few quiet knocks, sir, for I was feelin' fit to die.

Doctor (yelling). Aloysius! Oh, where's that rambling fool! Aloysius!

> [*Alleluia comes rushing in and over to the Doctor. He grips Jentree and pulls him into the circle again.*

Alleluia (to Jentree). Stand there; don't budge!

Doctor (furiously — to Alleluia). I'll budge you, you Poor Law Guardian's gett!

Alleluia (ignoring the Doctor — pulling the other patient to toe the line again). Stand there; don't budge!

Doctor (talking rapidly, pulling Alleluia by the coat to a place near the Surgery door). You stand there, and don't budge till they're all in and out again! (*To Jentree*) I told you not to come for a month. I gave you enough bromide mixture for a month. You're not going to die. Be off home.

Jentree. Yessir, nosir. But th' delugin' o' wather y'ordhered's doin' me no good.

Doctor. Take more of it, then, to weaken the wine in you. Now off you go. (*To the Young Woman*) You're Jenny Sullivan, aren't you?

Young Woman (with a prologue of a cough). Yessir.

Doctor (to Old Woman). What do you want — more liniment?

Old Woman. Yessir, please.

Doctor. Get it then, and go. (*Indicating Green Muffler*) Who's that man?

Alleluia (sliding into a bending position before the Doctor). A three-bottle man; a newcomer.

Doctor (calling down to him). Eh, you, come on in to me.

[*He returns to the Surgery.*

Jentree (as he goes out). Weaken th' wine in me! It's in an ambulance I ought to be, speedin' to a place where a qualified man ud be sacked if he left me out of his sight for a minute! I'll appeal to the authorities, so I will — this very day!

Old Woman. Arra, be sensible, son! Let what they give kill or cure us, there's ne'er a one for us to appeal to, bar the good God Himself! The poor who refuse to be patient, die young.

Red Muffler (fiercely). We've been too patient too long; too damned long; too god-damned long, I'm sayin'! Patience is only th' holy name for suicide!

> [*Alleluia glides along with Green Muffler to the Surgery door, ushers him in, and is about to close the door when the Doctor gives him a note.*

Doctor. Give that to Jenny Sullivan there, and tell her she can go.

> [*Alleluia gives the Young Woman the note. The Old Woman has crossed to the Dispensary window, handed in her prescription and bottle; received her liniment, and returned to the back to gaze out of the window at the falling snow.*

Old Woman (tonelessly). Th' snowy rain is worse nor what it was even.

Young Woman. Looka what I've got; looka what he's given me!

Old Woman. An' what is it, daughther?

Young Woman (tonelessly). A note to the Consumption Dispensary o' Charles Street. I'm done for now. I feel faint. I'll lose me job an' all, now. It's me death warrant!

Old Woman (coming over to her). Sit still for a few minutes, an' then we'll go home together. You'll have a lot more to go through before you'll be done for. There, sit still, child. I wouldn't say that he wasn't mistaken — th' fellow doesn't know black from white this mornin'. An' anyway, daughther, death's th' last thing th' poor should dhread.

[*A Lad of fifteen years of age comes into the waiting-room, and Alleluia at once glides down to him. The boy is thinly clad in coat and long trousers too big for him. His cap, too, is a size too large. He has the mask-like paleness of the others.*

Alleluia (*to the Lad*). What d'ye want?

Lad (*handing Alleluia a red ticket*). For me mother for the docthor to call.

Alleluia (*reprovingly*). Sir, sir; don't forget th' sir, lad. Are you workin'?

Lad. I deliver th' papers of a mornin'. I get two shillin's a week.

Alleluia. An' how much d'ye keep for yourself?

Lad. Fourpence.

Alleluia. Sir, sir; don't forget th' sir — where were you brought up? Don't you know your catechism?

Lad. Wha'?

Alleluia. Wha'! That's not th' way to addhress a superior. How much o' th' last fourpence have you left?

Lad. Tuppence, sir; only tuppence.

Alleluia. Ah, that's better. (*He shows the Lad the collecting-card.*) Remember th' Holy Souls. Put one o' th' pennies on th' card for th' Holy Souls.

[*After some hesitation, the Lad forks out a penny and gives it to Alleluia, who marks it down by pricking the card with a pin.*

Lad (*earnestly*). Me mother says, sir, she's very sick an' can't stir in th' bed, an' would th' docthor please hurry to her?

Alleluia (*almost shoving the Lad out*). Tell your mother that th' docthor'll go full gallop to her!

[*Green Muffler now comes from the Surgery and goes over to the Dispensary window. He planks his three bottles down on the ledge in front of the hand-out window, and then hands in his prescription to the Apothecary. Alleluia glides over to him, in the hope of collecting another penny for the Holy Souls.*

Alleluia (*archly holding collecting-card under Green Muffler's nose*). A penny to help the Holy Souls outa Purgatory, kind man o' th' three big bottles.

Apothecary's Voice (*at the window — to Green Muffler*). Take them bottles away.

[*Alleluia is startled; lowers card, and listens.*

Green Muffler (*startled and puzzled*). Eh? Wha'? What bottles?

Apothecary's Voice (*impatiently*). Them on th' ledge. (*Shouting*) Them on th' ledge!

[*Alleluia, scenting danger, glides away, and stands as close as he can get to the Surgery door.*

Green Muffler. I was ordered to bring three bottles. Th' person in authority here said I must have three bottles on me. Bring, says he, three bottles, says he, one for a liniment, one for a mixture, says he, an' one for a draught.

Apothecary's Voice (*impatiently*). Do what you're told, man! (*Shouting*) Take them outa the way! They're no use here!

[*Green Muffler takes the three bottles from the ledge and deposits them on the floor. After a moment or two, the Apothecary's hand puts a tiny box of pills on the ledge in front of Green Muffler. He is shocked, looking at the tiny box, and then at the bottles.*

Green Muffler (*to the patients — who keep a tense silence*). Did yous see what's after happenin'? Did yous or did yous not? Yous all saw me entherin' burdened with bottles, be

strict orders forced to spend me last penny to get them. An'
when I present them, as sthrictly ordered be a certain person,
I'm shouted at to take them away, an' even th' use of one was
denied me. (*He extends his hand with the tiny pill-box on its
palm.*) Looka what I got; just looka what I got! (*He comes
into the centre of the room.*) I'm not dhreamin', mind you.
This isn't fairyland either. Yous all seen what happened.
After all me huntin' after bottles, looka what's been handed
out! (*He glares towards where Alleluia is busy totting up what he
has collected on his card — ostensibly unaware of what is taking
place.*) Yous all heard what a certain person said to me. You
must have three bottles, he says, one for a mixture, one for a
liniment, he says, an' one for a draught. Three, mind you.
Yous all sung a song about the necessity for bottles. An' what
was the outcome? Yous all seen it yourselves. Yous all see the
bottles scattered about, an' me left with what's shinin' in th'
palm of me hand! I'm not dhreamin', mind you! Have yous
nothin' to say to relieve me feelin's? (*He moves towards the
door to go.*) Jasus, it's a cruel thing to do on anyone. (*He turns
to look towards the patients.*) An', mind you, that certain person
thried to cadge another penny off me for the Holy Souls! An'
what about th' sufferin' souls here, eh? (*He goes to the door, and
turns again.*) God forbid I'd ever come here again; but if I
have to, I warn that certain person not to mention bottles to
me; for if that certain person does, he'll be a sufferin' soul in
Purgatory himself, without a one to help him out!

> [*He goes slowly out, leaving the bottles on the floor beside
> the Dispensary; and, as he goes, he fixes his gaze on the
> pill-box.*

> [*The Doctor comes from the Surgery, dressed for the street
> as he was when we first saw him. He sees the patients
> sitting on the bench.*

Doctor (*calling*). Aloysius! (*Alleluia comes gliding up to him.*) Why are these still there? Why haven't they gone home?

Old Woman (*apologetically — to the Doctor*). The Young Woman here felt faint, an' we were restin' till she got a bit betther.

Doctor. She can't rest here. It's nearly closing time. The best place for her is home. (*To Old Woman*) Do you live near her?

Old Woman. Only a sthreet away, sir.

Doctor. Well, see her safe home, like a good woman. (*To Alleluia*) Close the house up, Aloysius. (*To Red Muffler who has come close to him*) What is it you want, and speak quick, for I'm in a hurry.

Red Muffler. It's me child, sir; me little girl, sir, only just nine years old.

Doctor. Yes, yes; what about her?

Red Muffler. We're afraid for her. You saw her four days ago; top room, hundhred an' one Hill Sthreet, sir. We want you to come at once.

Doctor. I know, I know; everyone wants the doctor to come at once. I'll come sometime tomorrow.

> [*The Doctor makes a step forward towards the entrance door, but Red Muffler makes one too, so that he stands somewhat in the way of the Doctor's passage to the door. At the same time, the Apothecary comes out of the Dispensary. He is dressed for the street — long mackintosh, thick white and red muffler, and a grey trilby hat pulled well down on his forehead. He carries an attaché-case and a walking-stick. He stands outside the Dispensary door and watches what is going on.*

Red Muffler (*blocking the Doctor's way to the door*). No, today, sir, please: now. She needs you now. Have a look at her, at least. Last night was one of agony to th' missus an' me, listenin' to her losin' her breath. We're afraid soon she'll silently be seen no more. She's bad; she's worse; she's chokin'!

Doctor. I'll go tomorrow; I can't go sooner. There are others needing attention, you know.

[*He goes to go, but Red Muffler catches his arm.*

Red Muffler (*desperately*). Nine years isn't long enough for a life to live! Damn it, man, if you've none for me, have some thought for th' mother watchin' th' child's rash sthruggles to live!

Doctor (*chucking his arm from Red Muffler's hold*). Oh, man alive, there are thousands of kids like yours gasping for life in the city today.

Red Muffler (*fiercely*). An' no-one seems to care a coloured damn about them!

Doctor. No living doctor can give them what they need, man. To worry about them would send me to the grave, too.

[*A young woman appears at the entrance door. Her head and half her body are covered by a grey shawl; her thin skirt is black, fading now to a rusty brown; her boots are old, and are sodden with the slush of the streets.*

Doctor (*seeing Grey Shawl — angrily to Alleluia*). Don't let any more in — put that one out!

[*Alleluia goes gliding down and tries to turn Grey Shawl back, but she pushes him roughly aside and hastens up to Red Muffler.*

[*The Doctor is now half-way down to the door; Red Muffler beside him, a little to his front; Grey Shawl in front of Red Muffler; the Old Woman and the Young Woman have risen from the bench, and stand behind to the left, almost directly in front of the poster warning of*

*Diphtheria. The Old Woman has an arm around the
young one, though she needs support herself. The
Apothecary stands a little in front of his Dispensary
door.*

Red Muffler (to Grey Shawl — frightened at seeing her).
What'r you doin' here? I had to wait to thry to get th' docthor.
Who's with th' child? Why th' hell did you leave her?

Grey Shawl (very quietly). You needn't throuble th' docthor
further, Frank. An' I didn't leave little Sheila, it was her who
left me.

[*Her hand steals forward to cling to a hand of Red
Muffler's, and there is a silence for some moments.*

Red Muffler (quietly). Well, we've got all we could get here,
so we'd betther go. (*To the Doctor*) You might have safely said
you'd come, an' kept hope danglin' still in front of us that
healin' still was here, an' common goodness. Our little one
has had th' charity to save you from a cold an' tirin' journey in
th' mornin'. (*Fiercely*) Oh, you blasted fomenter of medicine,
you might have listened to what I thried to say!

Grey Shawl (frightened). Frank! Do come home, an' don't
make a show of us an' little Sheila. I'm frightened she's feelin'
lonely wherever she may be now.

Old Woman (coaxingly). Ay, do, son, go home. Ah, it's
curious how th' old is left to wither on, while th' young often
go before they've time to bloom. It doesn't seem right to me.
I could ha' gladly gone in the little one's place; for head down
an' back bent, what's for me to thry to tarry here a minute
longer! God Almighty does odd things at times.

Grey Shawl (coaxingly). Come on, Frank, till you see her.
She's got all her old good looks back again. (*Brokenly*) Oh, me
little one'll be runnin' round frightened, lookin' for her
mammy, among the spirits of the blest!

Red Muffler (to the Doctor). D'ye hear that? She's got her old good looks all back again. Death has sometimes a kindlier touch than many a human hand.

> [*Red Muffler and Grey Shawl go out followed by the Old Woman and the Young Woman, who pass Red Muffler and Grey Shawl by as Red Muffler turns around at the door with a parting shot at the Doctor.*

Red Muffler (turning back at the door). The pair of yous can go home now, an' snore away some other buddin' life! Yous are afraid to fight these things. That's what's th' matther — we're all afraid to fight!

Apothecary (after a pause). Cheeky boyo, that! Not a grain of gratitude in one of them for all we thry to do for them. Well, I'll be off — good day. It would almost make a man despair of humanity! See you in th' morning.

Doctor. Good day. I hope so.

> [*The Apothecary goes off. Alleluia comes gliding down to the Doctor and holds out the red ticket given to him by the young Lad.*

Alleluia (holding out the ticket). Another visitin' ticket, sir.

Doctor (impatiently). Put it on my desk, put it on my desk, man! (*Alleluia glides off swiftly, with hand extended holding the red ticket; dives into the Surgery; comes out again, and watches the Doctor go. The Doctor pulls the white muffler closer around his neck, settles his hat more firmly on his head, giving a few thick coughs as he does so, and goes out of the waiting-room. Giving a richer belch as he goes out by the door.*) Jasus, I'm in a terrible state!

> [*Alleluia shuts the Surgery door and locks it, putting the key in his pocket. He goes to the Dispensary door and locks that too. He sees the three bottles on the floor that

Green Muffler left behind him. He takes them up and shoves them under the bench, singing the chorus of 'The Rose of Tralee' as he does these things. The organ is heard softly playing its old tune; it comes faintly into the room, as if to counterpoint the song sung by Alleluia.

Alleluia (singing, and breaking off at times, resuming again when his breathing finds it convenient):

She was lovelee an' fayer as ay . . . rose . . . bud in summer.

But it was not . . . her beau . . . tee aylone that won . . . me;

Ah, no, 'twas they trewth in her . . . eyes fondly beam . . . in',

That mayed me love Mary, they rose of

> [*He is now at the entrance door; he gives a last look round, then goes out, closing the door behind him. Outside the door*]

Traa . . . leee!

AS THE CURTAIN FALLS

THE ROSE OF TRALEE

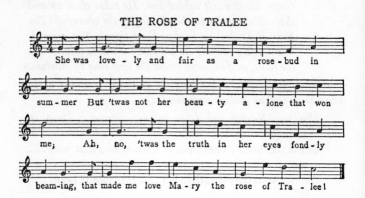

She was love-ly and fair as a rose-bud in sum-mer But 'twas not her beau-ty a-lone that won me; Ah, no, 'twas the truth in her eyes fond-ly beam-ing, that made me love Ma-ry the rose of Tra-lee!

ALLELUIA
Caretaker's Chant

All-all-e-*lui*-á   all-e-all-e-*lui*-á.
All-all-e-*lui*-á   all-e-all-e-*lui*-á.

BEDTIME STORY
An Anatole Burlesque in One Act

CHARACTERS IN THE PLAY

JOHN JO MULLIGAN, *a clerk*
ANGELA NIGHTINGALE, *a gay lass*
DANIEL HALIBUT, *a clerk—friend to Mulligan*
MISS MOSSIE, *a very respectable lodging-house keeper*
A POLICEMAN
A DOCTOR
A NURSE

———

SCENE

A bachelor-flat in Dublin.

TIME.—The present.

The sitting-room of the bachelor-flat rented by John Jo Mulligan from Miss Mossie, owner of one of the old houses of Dublin, decayed a little, but still sternly respectable, and kept presentable by her rigid attention to it. She has divided it into lodgings for respectable young gentlemen. A rather dull though lofty room. To the right is an ordinary gas fire; over it a mantelpiece on which is a clock, flanked on either side by a coloured vase; over these, on the wall, a square, gilt-framed mirror. Further up, towards back, is a door leading to Mulligan's bedroom. By the back wall, near this door, is a small bookcase with a few books sprawled out on its shelves; and on top is a pale-green vase holding a bunch of white pampas grass. To the left of this is a window, now heavily curtained with dull, brown hangings. In the window's centre is a stand holding a coloured flower-pot containing some kind of a palm plant. Further on is a picture of a whitewashed cottage, well thatched with straw, a brown pathway before the door, with purple heather growing in tufts on its edges, and, in the distance, the dark-blue peaks of hills, all surmounted by a bright blue sky. In the side wall on the left is the door leading to the rest of the house. On this door several overcoats are hanging. To the left of it is an umbrella-stand in which are a walking-stick and two umbrellas, one newer than the other. Close to the fireplace is an armchair clad in dark-green leather, and further away, at an angle, is a settee to hold two, clad in the same colour. In the room's centre is a round table covered with a red table-cloth. On the table are a photograph or two, a vase of chrysanthemums, and a book, open, with its face turned down, so that the place might not be lost when the reader left it aside. The room is lighted from a bulb hanging from the centre of the ceiling; the light is softened by being covered with a yellow parchment shade. A standard lamp stands on the floor a little way from the sitting-room door, towards the window, its light mollified by a deeply-fringed red silk shade. A key is sticking in the keyhole of the sitting-room door. A pair of Mulligan's tan shoes are beside the fireplace. It is three or four of a cold, sleety January morning.

The fire is unlit, the room in darkness, when, presently, the bedroom door opens, and Mulligan comes into the sitting-room, showing the way to himself by the light of an electric torch. He is but half dressed, in blue shirt, bright-checked, baggy plus-fours, and coloured-top stockings. He is a young man of twenty-four or -five; tall, but not thin. His hair is almost blond, and he wears it brushed back from his forehead, which is too high for the rather stolid face, giving him, at times, the look of a clown having a holiday. His upper lip has a close-cropped moustache. He is a constitutionally frightened chap, never able to take the gayer needs of life in his stride — though he would be glad to do it, if he could; but he can never become convalescent from a futile sense of sin. His clean-shaven face shows a very worried look. He comes into the room cautiously, waving the light over the floor, the table, the chairs, as if looking for something — as a matter of fact, he is; then returns to the door to peep into the bedroom.

Mulligan (sticking his head into the room — in a cautious whisper). I can't see the thing anywhere. Sure you left it out here? (*There is no reply to the question.*) I say I can't find it anywhere out here. (*There is no reply. He mutters to himself as if half in prayer*) I shouldn't have done it; I shouldn't have done it! I musta been mad. Oh, forgive me! (*He clicks his tongue, and peeps into the room again.*) Dtch dtch! Gone asleep again! (*Whispering*) Angela! Angela! (*In a louder whisper*) Are you awake? Eh, Angela?

Angela (within the room — sleepily). Wha'?

Mulligan (echoing her). Wha', wha'! (*To himself*) Oh, it was a mad thing to do. Miserere mei. (*Speaking into room with irritation*) Have you forgotten what you sent me out to get? (*Appealingly*) Please try to arouse yourself, Angela!

Angela (within). Wha'?

[*Silence again for a few moments while Mulligan flashes the light on to the clock.*

Mulligan. It's going to four o'clock in the morning, Angela.

Angela (within). Didja get the lipstick?

Mulligan (testily). I've told you I can't see it anywhere.

Angela (sleepily). Have another look — there's a dear. I know I left it out there somewhere.

Mulligan (shivering a little). It's nothing like a tropical climate out here, you know.

Angela (sleepily). It's easy to li' the fire, isn't it?

[*Mulligan crosses to the fireplace, turns the gas tap, and sees that the meter wants another shilling. He irritatedly turns the tap off, and, crossing quickly back to the bedroom, knocks over the vase of flowers on the table, sending the water spilling over the table and on to the floor.*

Mulligan (half to himself and half to Angela — with annoyance). There's the vase down! Wather into me shoes and all over the floor! (*Putting his head into the bedroom again*) I've knocked the vase down now! The place is flooded! And I can't light the fire — the meter needs another shilling.

Angela (sleepily). Look in me han'bag, somewhere about. Maybe there's a bob in it.

[*In desperation, Mulligan goes to the cupboard, opens it, takes out a wallet from which he takes a shilling, goes back to fireplace, puts it in the slot, and lights the fire. Then he returns to the bedroom door.*

Mulligan (putting his head into the bedroom again). Angela, are you up yet? The whole place is flooded. (*He gets no answer.*) You're not going asleep again, are you? Angela!

Angela (within — sleepily). What time is it?

Mulligan (in a loud and impatient whisper). I told you long ago. It's going to four o'clock in the morning. That friend of mine I told you of, will be back any minute from his all-night dance, before you slip away, if you don't hurry.

Angela (from within). And what if he is? If he knew what had been going on in here, he'd be sorry he ever went to the dance.

Mulligan. Looka, Angela, I don't feel a bit funny about it. We should never have done it. Please get up, and face the situation. Remember your solemn promise to slip off when things were still.

> [*Angela appears at the door. She is a girl of twenty-five to twenty-seven, tall, trimly-formed, and not without dignity. Her hair is auburn, inclining towards redness. She is something of a pagan.*

> [*At present, she is dressed in her cami-knickers, covered by Mulligan's brown dressing-gown, and her bare feet are thrust into Mulligan's slippers. Far and away too good a companion of an hour, a year, or a life, for a fellow like Mulligan.*

Angela (from the doorway). D'ye like the dark because your deeds are evil, or what? Switch on the light for God's sake, man, and let's have a look at each other before you banish your poor Eve from her Mulligan paradise.

Mulligan (as he switches on the light). I was afraid someone outside might see it, stay to look, might hear our voices, and wonder.

Angela. Wonder at what?

Mulligan. At hearing a girl's voice in my room at this time of night or morning.

Angela (mockingly). And isn't it a sweet thing for a girl's voice to be heard in a man's room at this time o' the night or morning?

Mulligan (almost tearfully). You know it's not; not as we're situated. You know you did wrong to practise on a body who didn't know enough. Situated as we are, without divine warrant, it's not proper. We're in the midst of a violent sin, and you should be ashamed and sorry, instead of feeling sinfully gay about it. It's necessary to feel sorry for a sin of this kind.

Angela. You were quite gay when we were coming in, boy, weren't you? You've had your few bright moments, and you've given a sparkle to your life, so don't spoil it all. It may well be more serious for me than it is for you. (*She shivers.*) Burr! It's cold here! I'll come back when the room's warmer, and make myself ready to meet the respectable world.

[*She goes back into the bedroom, while he stands at the bedroom door for a few moments, not knowing what to do.*

Mulligan (eyes raised appealing to the ceiling). Oh, that one'll be well punished for her gaiety and carelessness in sin! Oh, when will I forget this night's doings? Shattering fall! The very next day after me Novena too! (*He peeps into the bedroom.*) Don't get too cosy there, or you won't want to move. Move we must, and soon. (*He goes to the cupboard, relocks it, and puts the key in his pocket; then he goes to the armchair, sits down in it, and starts to put on his shoes. Putting on a shoe — in a half-prayer*) Sweet Saint Panteemalaria, get me outa this without exposure. (*He clicks his tongue*) Dtch dtch! Soaking wet! and I'll be a cautious goer from this out — I promise. (*He goes over to bedroom door again with but one shoe on, and peeps in.*) Angela, room's warm now; quite warm. The time's flying, mind you. (*There is no reply.*) Aw, God, have you gone to sleep again! Please, Miss Nightingale, please have some regard for others!

Angela (*from within — sleepily*). Did you find it?

Mulligan. Find what, find what?

Angela. Me lipstick you were looking for?

Mulligan. No, no, I didn't; must be in there somewhere.

Angela. I remember I had it when you had me perched on your lap. Remember?

Mulligan (*as if to someone in sitting-room*). Oh, don't be reminding me of things! (*Into the bedroom*) No, I don't remember. Oh, for goodness' sake, get up!

Angela. All right, all right. Put out a glass of wine, and I'll be out in a minute.

> [*Mulligan goes to the cupboard, unlocks it, and takes out a bottle of wine and a glass. He locks the cupboard again, leaving the key in the keyhole. He goes to the table, fills out a glass of wine, and leaves it, with the bottle, on the table, in readiness for Angela.*
>
> [*He sits down in the armchair, puts on the other shoe, then winds a woollen muffler round his neck, puts on a pull-over and coat that have been hanging over the back of a chair, and finally places a trilby hat on his head. As he does these things, he occasionally mutters to himself.*

Mulligan (*busy with the wine for Angela*). Not a single thought has she for what might happen to me if discovery came. Utterly abandoned to her own intherests. (*As he sits in chair putting on the second shoe — in a full-blown prayer*) Oh, gentle Saint Camisolinus, guardianess of all good young people, get between me and this petticoated demonsthrator of sinful delusion, and I'll be O.K. for evermore. I will, I promise!

*[Angela comes into the room at last, and makes quick for
the fire. She has put on her stockings — silk ones — and
skirt, a short, well-tailored one of darkish green, with
broad belt of dark red and black buckle. She carries a
brown jersey over her arm, and her shoes in her hand.*

*Angela (throwing her shoes on to the armchair, and stretching
her hands to the fire).* Burr! It's cold out here still! I thought
you said the room was warm? (*She notices how he's dressed.*)
All ready for the journey, eh? Soon we'll be skiing down the
stairs, wha'? Praying to all the saints you know to see me out, eh?

*[She puts the jersey on over her head before the mirror over
the fireplace, and pats it down smoothly over her breast
and shoulders.*

Angela. We have to face the hard, cold facts now, haven't we,
dear?

Mulligan. We've got to think now of what would become of
me if you were discovered here.

Angela (mockingly). Really? Of course, when one thinks of
it, that becomes the one important problem.

Mulligan (not noticing the mockery). It is, actually. You see,
Angela, the head of my department's a grand Knight of
Columbanus, an uncompromising Catholic, strict in his
thought of life, and if he heard of anything like this, I'd — I'd
be out in the bleaker air, quick; the little gilt I have on life
would be gone; I'd run to ruin! God help me!

Angela (prompting him). And then there's Father Demsey?

Mulligan. Then there's Father Demsey whose right-hand
man I am in the Confraternity and at all Saint Vincent de
Paul meetings, with his 'We can safely leave that matter with
Mr. Mulligan', or 'John Jo will do this for us'. You see, it's a
matter of importance to more than me. So, come on — we
bether get off at once.

Angela (*rising from the chair, and drinking the glass of wine*). Angela's bright eyes, her scarlet lip, fine foot, straight leg, and quivering thigh have lost their charm for Mr. Mulligan. He's all for go-ahead godliness now! (*She pours out another glass of wine and drinks it.*) And what is to become of me? You don't care, and I don't care either.

[*She moves about the room in a slow, semi-reckless rhythm as she lilts — Mulligan following her trying to get her quiet again.*

Angela (*lilting and moving about*):

I don't care what becomes of me,
I don't care what becomes of me.

Mulligan (*shuffling after her as she moves as well as he can — in a low, anguished voice*). Angela, please! Sit down, do!

Angela (*lilting*):

I don't care if I'm out till two,
I don't care for the man in blue.

Mulligan (*following her*). Please, Miss Nightingale, be serious! The landlady'll hear you, and then we'll be done!

Angela (*lilting*):

I don't care what the people say,
Here, there, and everywhere;

Mulligan (*appealing to the ceiling*). Saint Curberisco, help me!

Angela (*in a final burst*):

For I'm going to be married in the morning,
So tonight, boys, I don't care!

(*Facing towards Mulligan.*) Sometime or other, we have to face out of all we get into: face out of getting into bed with a woman no less than face out into silence from the glamour of prayer; face out of summer into winter; face out of life into death!

Mulligan (*crossing himself*). Your talk's near blasphemy, Angela! Now you're going where you shouldn't venture. You'll bring a curse down on me, if you're not careful! Please be more discreet.

Angela. They're facts.

Mulligan. We're not fit for facts now.

Angela (*facing him fiercely*). You stand there mustering up moans for yourself, and never once realise that you've ruined me! Yes, ruined me!

Mulligan (*startled*). Oh, God, d'ye hear her! Ruined you? Oh, come, now, don't thry to act the innocent.

Angela. It's you who's acting the innocent, but it won't work. I was only an innocent kid till I met you. You led me on and destroyed all confidence in the goodness of me own nature! You never, never ceased from persuasion till you got me here. I wasn't even to take off my hat, if I was the least bit suspicious. We were just to sit quiet discussing Yeats's poems. You were to sit ice-bound in your chair.

Mulligan (*indignantly*). I led you on! Angela Nightingale, you're inventing things. It was you insisted on coming, because you didn't like restaurants. A sorry thing for me I ever listened to you!

Angela (*ignoring his remarks*). It's me's the sorry soul for listening to you. You promised a quiet hour of poetry, but we were hardly here when you began to move. Yeats's poems soon flew out of your head and hand. You got as far as 'I will arise and go now, and go to Innisfree'; then before the echo of the line was hushed, you had me clapped down on your knee. (*She becomes tearful.*) That was the start of my undoing. What am I going to do!

Mulligan (*lifting his eyes to the ceiling*). There's lies! (*Facing her*) Astounded I was, when without a word of warning, I found you fitting into me lap! (*Coming closer to her — fervently*) The thruth is, if you want to know, that all the way to here, I was silently praying to a bevy of saints that you'd stay torpid in any and every emergency of look or motion!

Angela. You took care to leave your saints out on the doorstep; ay, and shut the door in their faces, too. You gave your solemn word, before I'd take one step to this place, that you'd be as harmless as an image in a looking-glass. I trusted you. I had heard you were a good boy. I thought you were a gentleman.

Mulligan. What about your uplifting can-can round the table while I was reading Yeats's poem?

Angela (*going her own way*). You made me believe you'd keep the width of a world between us while we were together, so's to avoid accidents. You said anyone who knew you would tell me you had a profound respect for girls; that you were slow in love-making.

Mulligan (*with insistence*). The can-can; what about the can-can around the table?

Angela (*with a great wail in her voice*). And then you stunned me with your speed!

Mulligan (*with greater insistence*). I'm asking you what about the can-can you danced around the table while I was thrying to read 'I will arise and go now, and go to Innisfree'?

Angela (*acting the innocent*). What can-can? What are you talking about? I don't know what you mean by can-can.

Mulligan. I mean the dance that uplifted your skirt out of the way of your movements and juggled a vision of spiritual desolation into a mirage of palpitating enjoyments.

Angela (*appealing to the world at large*). Oh, d'ye hear the like o' that! Meanness is most of you to try to put the cloak of your own dark way round my poor shoulders! The dance I did could be done by an innocent figure in a nursery rhyme.

You were bent on this awful mischief from the first. I sensed it when I walked with you — something evil hovering near. Oh, why didn't I follow me intuition! (*She begins to be hysterical.*) And I thought you such a nice man; and now, after fencing me in with shame, you're making out I gave you the stuff to make the fence around me. Oh, the infamy of it! (*She moves rapidly up and down the room, clasping and unclasping her hands.*) Oh, what shall I do, where shall I go, what shall I say!

Mulligan (getting very frightened). Angela, calm yourself. Speak lower, or you'll wake Miss Mossie, and we'll be ruined. Sit down; do, please!

Angela (fluttering about and staggering a little). I'm undone, undone completely. I won't be able to look any honest woman in the face; I won't be able to shake the hand of any honest man I meet; my future's devastated! (*She presses a hand to her heart.*) I'm not feeling well; not at all well; you'd better get Miss Mossie.

Mulligan (horrified and very agitated). Angela!

Angela (staggering towards the chair). Not well at all. I feel I'm going to faint! No, no; yes, yes — I am going to faint!

[*She sinks down on the chair, stretches out, and closes her eyes.*

Mulligan (falling on a knee before her — well frightened now). Angela, don't! Angela, dear, wake up! (*Lifting his eyes to the ceiling.*) Saint Correlliolanus, come on, and deliver us from utther desthruction!

Angela (plaintively and faintly). Wather!

Mulligan (panic-stricken). No, wine! (*He rises from his knee, pours out a glass of wine, and brings it to her.*) Oh, Angela, why did you let yourself get into such a state? Here, take it quietly in sips. (*As she drinks it*) Sip, sip, sip. That should do you good. Hope no one heard you. Miss Mossie sleeps with one ear cocked. (*He strokes her hand.*) You'll soon be all right, and able to slip away in a few minutes.

Angela (*noticing the ring on the hand stroking hers*). Pretty ring; garnet set in gold; precious garnet, didn't you say?

Mulligan (*none too sure of what he should say*). Yep. Not much value though.

Angela. Why's it on the little finger?

Mulligan. Knuckle's too big on the right one; won't go over it.

Angela (*fingering it*). Let me see it in me hand. (*He hesitates, then takes it off, and gives it to her with reluctance. Putting it on the engagement finger*) Fits me to a nicety. How did you come by it?

Mulligan. An uncle left it in my care when he went on a job to Hong Kong. He never came back, and as no one asked about it, I made it my own.

Angela. Oh? Lucky one. (*She looks up into his face, smiling archly, displaying the finger with the ring on it*) Looks like we were an engaged couple, John Jo, dear, wha'?

Mulligan. An engaged couple? (*With an uneasy and constrained laugh*) Yis! Funny thought, that; quite. Feeling betther?

Angela. Seem to; hope it won't come over me again.

Mulligan (*fervently*). God forbid! What about taking off our shoes, and making a start?

[*He takes off his.*

Angela (*taking off her shoes*). I suppose we must go sometime.

Mulligan (*trying to speak carelessly*). Let's have the ring back, dear.

Angela (*as if she'd forgotten it*). The ring? Oh, yes; I near forgot. (*She fiddles with it; then suddenly straightens herself to listen.*) Is that the sound of someone at the door below?

Mulligan (*agitated again*). Oh God, if it's Halibut home from the dance we'll have to wait till he settles down! I wish you'd gone when the going was good!

Angela (*who has taken off her shoes — rising from the chair*). Come on, we'll chance it!

Mulligan (*pushing her back*). Chance it! We can't afford to chance it. (*Going over to the door leading to rest of the house*) I'll reconnoitre down, and make sure the way's clear, before we chance it.

> [*He goes out of the room, is absent for a few moments, while Angela swallows another glass of wine; then he returns hastily, a hand held up warningly for silence.*

Mulligan (*in a frightened whisper*). Near ran into him on the stairs. Thank God it was so dark. Just had time to turn back. We'll have to wait now till he settles in. (*He listens at the door, shuts it suddenly, and glides over to Angela.*) Quick! He's gone by his own place, and is coming up here! (*He catches her by the arm, hurries her across the room, and shoves her into the bedroom.*) Get in, and keep silent for God's sake!

> [*As he shoves her in, a knock is heard at the sitting-room door. Mulligan shuts the bedroom door, slides over to the chair, sits down, takes the book from the table, and pretends to be reading.*

> [*Another knock is heard at the door, then it opens, and Mr. Daniel Halibut is seen standing there. He is a man of twenty-five, a little below medium height, inclining to be plump. His hair is reddish, and a thick moustache flowing from his upper lip hides his mouth. Sometimes his hand tries to brush it aside, but the moment the hand is removed, it falls back into its old place at once. A*

*fawn-coloured overcoat covers an informal evening-suit
— dinner-jacket and black tie. A black homburg hat is
on his head. He comes in as one who is full of himself as
if he had done himself well at the dance, and as one who
feels himself a man of the world above the cautious and
timorous Mulligan. His hat and coat are damp.*

Halibut (coming into the room). Ha, there you are, me son,
rotten night out; sleet. Coming up, I could have sworn I seen
you coming down the stairs.

Mulligan (in pretended surprise). Me coming down the stairs?
At this time of the morning? What would I be doing on the
stairs at this hour?

Halibut. Well, what are you doing up at this time of the
morning?

Mulligan. I found it impossible to sleep, so got up to see if a
bit of Yeats's poetry would make me drowsy.

Halibut. Is it Yeats, is it? God, man, he wouldn't let you
sleep; drive you nuts! All people liking Yeats are all queer.
He's all questions. What am I? Why am I? What is it? How
did it come? Where will it go? All bubbles. Stuck up in the
top of his ould tower, he sent the bubbles sailing out through a
little loophole to attract the world outside. And all the little
writers copied them, and blew bubbles of their own, till you
could see them glistening among the things of the althar, or
shining in the hair of the girl you were courting.

Mulligan (with an obvious yawn). Well, Yeats has made me
sleepy, anyway. *(He flings the book on the table, and goes to get
out of the chair.)* I'll be off to bed again.

Halibut (shoving him back into the chair). Wait till I tell you.
You should ha' been at the dance. There never was a grander
occasion; divel a grander ever! The place was fair gushing with
girls. And only a few who'd make you shut your eyes if they

were sitting on your knee. A hilariously hopeful whirlwind of skirt and petticoat, John Jo, when a waltz was on!

Mulligan (getting up and edging Halibut towards the sitting-room door). Go to bed, now, like a good fellow. I'm tired. We'll talk about it tomorrow. Goodnight.

Halibut (edging Mulligan back towards the fireplace). Wait till I tell you. You are a boyo. You'd never guess who was there? Your old flame of a week — Jessie! She told me things! When will you wake up? When he asked me out for the first time, says she, I expected a hilarious night at a dance or a music-hall, says she; I near fainted, says she, when, instead, he asked me to go with him to Benediction! Mulligan's management of maidens! Oh, John Jo, when will you wake up?

Mulligan (annoyed, pushing Halibut towards the door). If I elect to keep from danger, that's my affair. Looka, Dan, I've got to get up early to go to Mass on my way to the office, so be a good fellow, and go. I'm not concerned with girls.

Halibut. Betther if you were. (*He pushes Mulligan back toward the fireplace again.*) You'd sleep betther at night for one thing. (*He puts an arm around Mulligan and forces him into being a partner.*) Roamin' in th' gloamin', eh? Oh, boy! (*Lilting*) With a lassie by yeer side. Oh, it's lovely to go roamin' in th' gloamin'!

Mulligan (angrily — struggling from Halibut's hold, and rather roughly forcing him to the door). Aw, lay off it, damn it, Dan! I'm in no mood for a Highland fling! Please go to your own room, and leave me in peace — I'm done in!

[*He shoves him out and closes the sitting-room door.*

Halibut (as he's being shoved out). All right, if that's the way you feel. It'd be a good thing to put your hand on a girl's knee, and chance it.

[*Mulligan listens at the door for a few moments. Then he gets down on his knees, and puts an ear to the floor. He rises, goes to the bedroom door, opens it, and calls Angela out.*

Mulligan. Now, Angela; now's our time. No delay, please.

Angela (*going behind the curtains on the windows*). What kind of a night or morning is it? (*From behind the curtains*) Mother o' God! It's snowing or something! (*She comes from behind them, goes to the door, and takes one of Mulligan's coats hanging there.*) I must have a coat.

[*Angela puts the coat on.*

Mulligan (*in a faint protest*). Eh, Angela, that's me best one.

Angela (*taking an umbrella from the stand*). And an umbrella, too.

Mulligan. That's me best umbrella.

Angela. Never mind, dear. I'll let you have it back when you hand me into the taxi on the all-night rank. Let's hurry now, boy. (*Mulligan opens the door cautiously, listens a moment; takes a torch from a pocket, and shines it forth, then leads the way from the room, shutting the door gently behind him. Both of them are in their stockinged feet. After a few moments have passed, the door suddenly flies open, and Angela hurries in, followed by Mulligan wearing a look of agony on his face. They carry their shoes under their arms. As she comes in*) You louser, you'd have let me go off without it! Didn't care a damn once you were rid of me. And all I have for another fortnight is in that handbag!

Mulligan (*appealingly*). Speak lower, Angela, or you'll have the Mossie one down on top of us! I just can't remember you having a handbag when you first came in.

Angela (*angrily*). You can't remember! Well, I had one, and a good one, too, and I've got to get it — see! D'ye mean to hint I'm making it up?

Mulligan (in agony). No, no; but for God's sake, speak easy; please, Angela!

Angela (leaving her shoes down, and pulling the cushions off the settee and throwing them on the floor). Well, then, find it for me. Mind you, had I been down the street when I missed it, I'd have banged the door down to get in to get it!

Mulligan (leaving his shoes down, and pulling the table about, pulling the chairs from the wall, and pulling the umbrella-stand away, to look behind them). This is terrible! I'll be ruined if I'm discovered. What colour was it? Where had you it last? Where d'ye think you could have put it?

Angela. I don't know, fool. It was a dark-green one I bought last week, and gave five pounds for. I got confused and forgot about everything when you started to pull me on to your knee.

Mulligan. But we can't stay to look for it. Miss Mossie'll soon be going about with her candle in her hand.

Angela. I'm not going without it! I think I remember you snatching it outa me hand when you started to pull me on to your lap.

Mulligan. Oh, give over about me pulling you on to me lap, and give us a hand to look for it! (*He runs into the bedroom, and starts to search there, flinging the bedclothes about. In bedroom*) I can't see it anywhere here, so I can't.

Angela (tearfully) And I was to come here only for a quiet glass of wine and a biscuit. That's what you said, and kept repeating; and I believed you, oh, I believed you!

Mulligan (coming out of bedroom). No sign of it there.

Angela (marching up and down the room, clasping and un-clasping her hands). Oh, isn't this a nice end to a quiet glass of wine and a biscuit!

Mulligan. Get a hold of yourself. What sort was it?

Angela. A pure morocco leather one, dark green, with initials on it filigreed in mother o' pearl.

Mulligan (*impatiently*). Yis, yis; (*anxiously*) but how much was in it altogether?

Angela. Fifteen pounds odd.

Mulligan (*aghast*). Good Lord!

Angela. And the lipstick you couldn't find musta been in it too; silver-cased and all; and a lovely bracelet watch waiting to be mended. Oh, what will I do! Oh, yes, and a silver brooch I wanted to get a pin for. What will I do, what will I do?

Mulligan. You slip off, and when I come back, I'll search high and low for it.

Angela (*with rising nervous tension*). And how am I to fare till you find it? You wouldn't turn a hair if I was willing to go in my shift! John Jo Mulligan, you're a dasthard! It would be the price of you to let Miss Mossie and the whole house know the sort you are!

Mulligan. For God's sake, Angela! What d'ye want me to do; only tell me what you want me to do?

Angela (*moving about distracted*). And to think I thought I was safe with you! (*Her glance falls on the cupboard, and she makes a bee-line for it*) Could it have got in here?

Mulligan (*hastily*). No, no; it couldn't have got in there.

Angela (*drawing out a leather wallet*). What's this?

Mulligan (*going over to take wallet from her*). Nothing there but a few private letters, and a lot of bills.

[*But before he can reach her to get it away, she has whisked a bundle of notes from it.*

Angela (*giggling — a little hysterical*). John Jo's hidden treasure. (*She counts them rapidly.*) Eighteen pounds ten. All fresh ones too. Nice to handle.

Mulligan. They're not mine. I'm minding them for a friend. You can put them back.

Angela (*mockingly*). At once, dear. I'll mind them for you, dear. (*She takes a cheque-book out of the wallet.*) A cheque-book, too. (*As he comes closer*) Keep your distance, keep your distance, or I'll claw the gob off you!

Mulligan. I was only going to give you a few of them to tide you over, dear.

Angela (*fiercely*). You were? How sweet of you! I'll have them all, you primly-born yahoo. And more. (*She raises her voice*) And more!

Mulligan (*whispering*). All right, all right, only keep calm; keep quiet.

Angela (*indicating the cheque-book*). Make me out a cheque for five pounds like a decent, honest man.

Mulligan (*taking a fountain pen from his pocket, and settling down to write*). All right; anything to pacify you.

Angela (*patronisingly patting his head*). You're not the worst, John Jo. You're really a pleasant chap when you get going. Make a cheque out for ten, darling, to compensate for the goods in the handbag. Ten, dear; that's all now. Well, we've had a right good time together. Pity I can't stay longer. See you again soon, when you're feeling frisky, eh? Naughty boy! (*She has taken the cheque from the dazed Mulligan, put it in his wallet, and now straightens herself to go, taking her shoes off the floor, and putting them under an arm. At the door*) I know my way down, so don't you stir. I'll steal away like a maid of Araby. I'll be seeing you. Be good.

[*Dazed and stunned, Mulligan sits still for a few seconds; then he gets up from the chair to look around him.*

Mulligan (*rising from the chair*). Fully-fledged for hell, that one, and you never noticed it! Oh, John Jo, John Jo! (*He suddenly stiffens.*) She had no handbag! She never had a handbag! Oh, Mother o'God, she's codded me! (*He looks in the cupboard, then looks over the table.*) She's taken away me wallet, too! Me umbrella!

> [*He runs out of the room to follow her, so agitated that he leaves door wide open behind him. There are a few moments of silence; then Miss Mossie appears at the open door with a lighted candle in a candlestick in her hand. She is a short, stout woman of thirty-five or so. She is dressed in a brown skirt reaching to her ankles, and we get a glimpse of black stockings sinking into a pair of stout black shoes. Her dark hair is gathered into a knob, and made to lie quiet on the nape of her neck. She wears a yellow jumper, and a brown Jaeger topcoat is flung over her shoulders. She wears spectacles. She looks into the room for a moment, a look of perplexed anxiety on her face, then turns aside to call to Halibut.*

Miss Mossie. Mr. Halibut, Mr. Halibut, come up, come up quick! (*Halibut appears at the door. He is now wearing a pair of blue pyjamas, covered by a dressing-gown of dark red, and his bare feet are slippered.*) Oh, Mr. Halibut, what can the matter be? Oh, dear, what can the matter be?

Halibut (*agog with excitement*). What's up, Miss Mossie?

Miss Mossie (*coming into the sitting-room, followed by Halibut*). Looka the state of the room; and Mr. Mulligan's just run out into the street in his stockinged feet!

Halibut (*astonished*). No? How d'ye know he went out into the street?

Miss Mossie. I seen him go. I heard something stirring when I was putting on me jumper, so I looked out, and there was Mr. Mulligan scuttling down the stairs. Walking in his sleep, he musta been. He had an air on him as if he was enraptured within himself; a look as if he was measuring life and death together to see which was tallest.

Halibut. Is that right? Coming back from the dance, I thought I saw him on the stairs, too, but when I came up, he was sitting reading Yeats's poems. Said he couldn't sleep. I warned him against the poems.

Miss Mossie (coming over to the bedroom door, and opening it). Oh, looka the state of this room, too! Everything flung about.

Halibut (awed). Looks like he had a wild fit, or something!

Miss Mossie. Something terrific! This isn't just disarray, Mr. Halibut — it's an upheaval! You don't think it could be that something suddenly went wrong in him?

Halibut (startled by a thought). Wrong in him, Miss Mossie? What could go wrong in him?

Miss Mossie. A quietly-disposed man like Mr. Mulligan doesn't do this (*indicating disorder of rooms*) without something whizzing within him.

Halibut (frightened). You mean in his mind?

Miss Mossie (firmly). We must act. We can't let him roam the streets or do any harm here. I'll phone the police and a doctor, and I'll slip out for the constable that usually stands at the street corner. (*They move to the sitting-room door.*) I'll go now. You stay on the lobby here in the dark, and watch over him if he comes back.

Halibut (dubiously). I'm not a strong man, Miss Mossie.

Miss Mossie. After all, Mr. Halibut, we don't want to be murdhered in our beds.

Halibut (crossing himself). God forbid, Miss Mossie!

Miss Mossie. And the odd thing is, he'd be doing it with the

best intentions. If he comes back, he may still be asleep, so
don't shout at him and wake him too suddenly. Just humour
him, unless he gets violent.

Halibut (picturing in his mind all that might happen). Ay,
violent — that's the danger!

Miss Mossie. Then you'll just have to close with him, and
hold him till the constable comes.

Halibut (panic-stricken). Close with him? Hold him till the
constable comes? But, woman alive, I'm not gifted that way!

Miss Mossie. You'll do your best, I know; if he overcomes
you, it won't be your fault.

Halibut. Don't you think it would be only prudent to have a
poker handy?

Miss Mossie. Too violent-looking. (*Indicating a corner of the
lobby*) There's the bit of curtain-pole I use to push the window
up — you can keep that handy; but don't let him guess why
you have it. (*She takes the key from the inside and puts it in the
keyhole on the outside of the door*) There now, if the worst
comes, you can fly out and lock him safely within the room.

Halibut. It sounds easy, but it's really a desperate situation.

Miss Mossie. Don't let him see you're frightened. Keep him
under command. That's what me sisther did with me when I
used to walk in my sleep a few years ago.

Halibut (stricken with confused anxiety). What, you used to
sleep-walk, too?

Miss Mossie. That's why I dhread the habit coming back to
me, for then you never know whether you're always asleep
and never awake, or always awake and never asleep. I'll be off
now. You'll be quite safe if you only keep your wits about you.

[*She goes off with her candle, leaving a world of darkness
to poor Halibut. There is a silence for a few moments,*

then the watcher in the darkness, and any who are
listening, hear a patter of feet on stairs outside, and the
voice of Mulligan calling out loudly the name of Miss
Mossie several times. Then a great bang of a closing
door; dead silence for a moment, till Mulligan is heard
calling again.

Mulligan (outside). Dan, Dan, are you awake? Dan Halibut,
are you awake, man? (*Mulligan appears on the lobby just outside*
the sitting-room door. He is talking to himself, a haggard, lost,
and anxious look on his face, and he is a little out of breath. His
coat and hat are damped by the falling sleet outside; his feet wet.
He pauses on the lobby, and waves his electric torch about till its
beam falls on the silent and semi-crouching Halibut.) Oh, it's
here you are? Thought you were in bed fast asleep. Called
you, but got no answer. What a night! Twenty-eight pounds
ten gone with the wind! (*He lifts a cushion from the floor to*
look under it.) It's not there! (*He flings it viciously away. To*
Halibut) What has you here in the dark and the cold?

Halibut. Just shutting the window to keep it from rattling.

Mulligan (going into the sitting-room). We must do something.
Miss Mossie's gone rushing hatless out into the darkness and
the sleet. Hatless, mind you! Looked as if she was sleep-walking again. A one-time habit of hers, did you know? You'll have
to go after her.

Halibut (coming a little way into the room, but staying close to
the door, holding the sprig of curtain-pole behind his back). I
know, I know; but what were you doing out in the sleet and
the darkness *yourself*? And in your stockinged feet, too, look
at them!

Mulligan. Me? Couldn't sleep; felt stifled; went out for
some fresh air. Didn't think of shoes. Something whizzing in
me mind. (*A little impatiently*) But you dress and go after

Mossie. See what's wrong with her. Several times, before you came, she came into my room, fast asleep, at dead of the night, with a loving look on her face. We can't afford to let ourselves be murdhered in our sleep, Dan. (*He flops into chair.*) Saint Fairdooshius, succour me this night.

Halibut (*bewildered with anxiety, eyes lifted to ceiling in a low appeal*). Oh, sweet Saint Slumbersnorius, come to me help now! (*To Mulligan*) All right; yes. I'll settle you in first. You go to bed, John Jo, quiet. Go to bed, go to bed, and go asleep, and go asleep!

Mulligan (*looking at Halibut curiously — a little impatiently*). I've told you I can't sleep. Twenty-eight pounds ten, and my fine leather wallet gone forever!

Halibut (*in a commandingly sing-song way*). Never mind. Put them out of your thoughts, and go to bed, go to bed, and go to sleep, and go to sleep — I command!

Mulligan (*half rising from his chair so that Halibut backs towards the door — staring at Halibut in wonderment*). What's wrong with you, Halibut? (*He sinks back into the chair again, and Halibut returns into the room.*) Me best coat and best umbrella, too! Gone.

> [*His glance happens to fall on his hand, and he springs out of the chair with a jump, sending Halibut backing swiftly from the room again.*

Mulligan. Me ring! I never got it back!

Halibut (*straying cautiously back into the room again*). Money, best coat, best umbrella, wallet, and ring! When did you lose all these things, man?

Mulligan. A minute or so ago; no, no, an hour ago; two hours ago; more. (*He leans his arms dejectedly on the table, and buries his head on them.*) I di'n't lost them, Dan; I gave them away, flung them all away!

Halibut. In an excess of charity of having too many possessions, or what? You know, I've warned you, John Jo; often warned you.

Mulligan (raising his head from his arms — resentfully and suspiciously). Warned me? How warned me?

Halibut. I warned you that running out to devotions morning and night, and too much valuable time spent on your knees, would upset you one day or another. And, now, you'll have to admit that these things couldn't have happened to you if you had had a girl with you tonight.

Mulligan (with a wail of resentment). Oooh! Don't be a blasted fool! (*He notices that Halibut has something behind his back.*) What's that you have behind you?

Halibut (trying to be carelessly funny). Me tail. Didn't you know? I'm a wild animal (*He wags the piece of curtain-pole.*) Now, the wild animal says you're to go to bed, go to bed, and go to sleep, and go to sleep. Obey the wild animal at once!

Mulligan (slowly rising from the chair, staring anxiously and suspiciously at Halibut). What's amiss with you, Halibut? Are you sleep-walking, too? Leave down that curtain-pole. Don't be acting the goat, man. (*Coaxingly — as Halibut brings the piece of curtain-pole to his front*) Go on, Dan, oul' son, leave the thing down!

Halibut. As soon as you're safely settled in bed, John Jo. Then I'll pop out after Mossie. To bed; to bed; and go to sleep, go to sleep — I command!

Mulligan (fear having come on him — suddenly seizes the wine-bottle by the neck, and holds it as a club, running to window, swinging back the curtains, and trying to open it). God Almighty, I'm alone with a lunatic! (*Shouting — as he tries to open the window*) Help!

Halibut. I'll not let you destroy yourself — come away from that window, or I'll flatten you!

Mulligan (*wheeling round, still holding bottle by the neck to use it as a club, and facing towards Halibut*). Looka, Halibut, leave that club down. (*Coaxingly*) Now, be sensible, Dan, like a good chap, and drop that club.

Halibut. Drop that bottle first, I say; drop that bottle first!

Mulligan. Drop that club, I tell you. (*Fiercely*) Drop that club!

Halibut (*dancing up and down — panic-stricken*). Put that bottle down! Put it down, and go to bed, I tell you!

Mulligan (*dodging about*). Drop that club at once, Halibut!

Halibut. Put that bottle down immediately!

Mulligan. I command you!

Halibut. I command you!

> [*They have been dodging about without coming near to each other; Halibut swinging the piece of curtain-pole to and fro in front of him for protection. In one of the blind swings, the pole slips from his hand, and sails out through the window, causing a great sound of falling glass. They both stare at the window — dumbfounded for a few moments.*

Mulligan (*exultingly*). Aha, I've got you now!

> [*But Halibut has fled from the room, banged the door after him, and locked it from the outside. Mulligan hurries to the door and presses his back to it. Then Miss Mossie's voice is heard outside.*

Miss Mossie (*outside*). Oh, what's happened? I feared it would end in violence! Mr. Halibut, Mr. Halibut, are you much hurted?

Mulligan (*shouting through the door to Miss Mossie*). Miss Mossie; here, Miss Mossie!

Miss Mossie (from outside). Oh, Mr. Mulligan, what have you done to poor, innocent Mr. Halibut? We've found him lying in a dead faint out here on the lobby.

Mulligan (indignantly — shouting outwards). Poor, innocent Mr. Halibut! What has he not tried to do to me! He rushed in here, lunacy looking out of his eyes, and tried to shatther me with a club, with a club; tried to murdher me! Now he's locked me in.

Miss Mossie (soothingly). Now isn't that a shame! What a naughty man he is! Never mind now. You go to your chair and sit down by the fire, and I'll get the key to open your door. Everything will be all right, Mr. Mulligan.

Mulligan (indignantly). Everything isn't all right now! I'll live no longer in the same house with Halibut!

Miss Mossie (coaxingly). Do go and sit down by the fire, Mr. Mulligan, there's a dear. I'll bring you a hot drink, and we'll talk about things; do, now, like a good man (*Mulligan goes to the fireplace, and sits down in the armchair. He lights a cigarette and puffs it indignantly. After a few moments, the door opens, and Miss Mossie lets into the room a big, topcoated and helmeted policeman, the doctor with his case, wearing an anxious look on his face, and a nurse, enveloped with a dark-blue cloak on the left side of which is a white circle surrounding a large red cross. She carries the usual nursing-suitcase in her hand. Miss Mossie is in the midst of them, and Halibut, in the rear, with a ghastly pale face, rises on his tiptoes to gaze over their shoulders. All but Halibut form a semicircle round Mulligan's back, who puffs away, unconscious of the entrance of the crowd. Bending sidewise from behind the policeman to speak to the sitting Mulligan*) Now, Mr. Mulligan, we'll see what all this little disturbance was about, and what was the cause of it, and then we'll be all — er — O.K., eh? And I've brought in a few kind friends to help me.

Mulligan (rising from his chair in blank surprise, and almost echoing Miss Mossie). A few friends to help you? (*He turns around to face Miss Mossie, but is confronted by the big, helmeted policeman, the doctor, and the nurse. He slides back into the chair almost in a dead faint. Falling back into the chair*) Good God!

CURTAIN

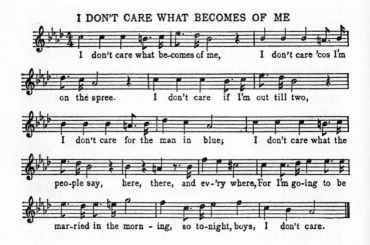

I DON'T CARE WHAT BECOMES OF ME

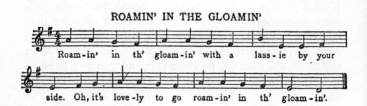

ROAMIN' IN THE GLOAMIN'

TIME TO GO
A Morality Comedy in One Act

CHARACTERS IN THE PLAY

MICHAEL FLAGONSON, *proprietor of a tavern*
BULL FARRELL, *proprietor of a general stores*
MRS. FLAGONSON, *Flagonson's wife*
BARNEY O'HAY, *farmer owner of five acres*
COUSINS, *farmer owner of twenty acres*
CONROY, *farmer owner of a hundred and fifty acres*
SERGEANT KILLDOOEY, *of the Civic Guards*
1ST CIVIC GUARD
2ND CIVIC GUARD
WIDDA MACHREE, *who has asked too much for a cow*
KELLY FROM THE ISLE OF MANANAUN, *who has given too little for it*
A YOUNG MAN
A YOUNG WOMAN

———

SCENE

Outside of Flagonson's Tavern and Bull Farrell's General Stores on the edge of an Irish country town, a day or so after a fair.

TIME.—The present.

The scene is the butt-end of an Irish town, small and untidy. To the left, part of Flagonson's Tavern façade can be seen. There are the door and a window to the right of it; the roof is of slate, and a smoke-grimed chimney is sending out a little trickle of smoke. Over the doorway is a notice declaring that BEER AND SPIRITS FOR ALL *can be had there; between the window and the door is a larger notice holding the printed announcement on it of* LUNCHES, DINNERS, AND TEAS — AD LIB; *the Latin phrase done out in larger letters. The front wall is brickwork half-way up, the rest is covered with a patchy rough-cast. A little way from the door are a rough wooden bench and a few kitchen chairs; and a few tankards stand on the table.*

Opposite to the Tavern stands the General Stores of Mr. Bull Farrell, jutting out far enough to show the wide doorway, a window, and part of the front wall. Along the wall is a board having on it the words BULL FARRELL. GENERAL STORES. FROM A NEEDLE TO AN ANCHOR. *Arranged along the wall, leaning against it, are a new hoe, a dung-fork, a spade; in front of them a new wheelbarrow, a dust-bin, a large box, and an eight-stone sack of phosphate. On the slated roof is a smoke-begrimed chimney from which ascends a little trickle of smoke.*

Beyond these two establishments is a road going across, and smaller ways lead past in front of the Tavern and the General Stores. In the background is a scrubby field with a vista of a few cottages, thatched, in the distance. On the edge of the field, close to the edge of the road, are the remains of two trees, one near the Tavern and the other near the General Stores. Their branches are withered, and they look as if they had been blasted by lightning. A string of various-coloured bunting, triangular in shape, connects Tavern and Stores, and a tiny string of the same bunting hangs over the Tavern door and over the door of the General Stores. Each has a small Papal flag, perpendicular stripes of white and yellow, stuck out from the upper part of the windows.

Over all is a lovely magenta-coloured sky, fleeced here and there by clouds, rosily-silver wherever the sun touches them.

Flagonson is standing by the edge of the table, his arse leaning against it. He is a man of fifty-five, big-headed, and strongly built. His hair, once a brilliant red, is now badly chaffed with grey. Although his belly is beginning to advance too far into the world, he is a well-formed, upstanding man. He is mechanically wiping a tankard with a cloth.

Bull Farrell, owner of the General Stores, is very different from Michael Flagonson. He is a wisp of a man, looking as if a shove would send him with speed flying out of the world. Although but forty years of age, he is quite bald, but his upper lip clings on to a thick, dark, truculent moustache. He is dressed in tweeds, and has a high, stiff, white collar round his neck, encircled with a black tie. A dark-blue apron protects his trousers from dust damage. Flagonson too wears a collar, not quite so high as that worn by Farrell; a low-necked dark waistcoat, with white front, and a black bow nestling under the stuck-out wings of the collar. His apron is a white one. Bull Farrell is standing in his doorway looking towards Flagonson.

Flagonson (*with a glance at the decorations*). How lonesome an' woebegone the decorations look now the crowd's gone.

Bull (*glancing at them, too*). Ay, with the coloured booths, the shoutin' of buyin' and sellin', the swearin' an' fightin' gone with th' crowd too, it's a bit lonely like. (*He glances at the decorations again.*) I dunno why you put them up. Waste of time; waste of money.

Flagonson (indicating those over Bull's door). You've a token hangin' there yourself.

Bull. Me great-grandfather bought them for some meetin' in honour of Dan O'Connell. They cost me nothin'.

Flagonson. An' what about the Papal flag?

Bull (gloatingly). I nailed that off a kid bangin' the window with it to th' point of breakin'; and when I threatened the police on him, he was damned glad to get away without it.

Flagonson. The polis is the only ones to put th' fear o' God in them.

Bull. Only for them, they wouldn't leave a thing standin' in th' town. Durin' th' Fair, they had me plagued. I daren't ha' left a thing standin' outside, or it would have been gone while I was winkin'.

Flagonson. Well, it's all cold an' calm now, anyhow. Nothin' left of all the burly business but big farmer Conroy an' little farmer Cousins still arguin'. Cousins wants to sell an' Conroy says he wants to buy, though, afther twelve hours of talkin', they're no nearer to an agreement yet.

Bull (coming from the door, and leaning towards Flagonson — confidently). Conroy sees somethin' in them cattle, though no-one else can. Conroy's a cute one. He says he wants only to do a good turn to poor Cousins. *(He throws back his head, and gives a loud guffaw.)* Conroy doin' a good turn! He's takin' a helluva time to do it. Slow, but sure!

Flagonson. I dunno. Maybe he has a soft spot in him somewhere.

Bull (with surprised indignation). Soft spot? Why, man alive, Conroy ud take the gold from a holy saint's halo an' shove it in th' bank!

Flagonson (after a pause). I wondher what happened to that fine-lookin' woman in th' black dhress and the bright blue cloak thryin' to sell her cow to th' upstandin' chap in the saffron kilt an' th' gay, green shawl?

Bull. She sold it all right to him, Barney O'Hay was tellin' me; an' then she went east an' he went west, leadin' th' cow home.

Flagonson. It wasn't what you'd call a bulky Fair. I've seen betther, an' I've seen worse.

Bull. So've I; but you musta made a bundle, seein' the house was packed all th' day an' half-way into th' night.

Flagonson (a little sharply, touched with envy). An' isn't the sufferin' road out there worn away with the constant caravan of donkey-cars, pony-cars, an' motor-cars, loaded to th' brims, carryin' off stuff from your stores, so that you musta been ladlin' money into your positive possessions!

Bull (placatingly). Don't grudge me mine, Mick, an' I won't grudge you yours.

Flagonson (cheerily). God forbid I did, Bull, for it wouldn't be a Christian thing to do. Though me own takin's timidly topped last year's, I'd say I never seen a quieter Fair: all noise, a noise of bargainin', with a little laughter an' gaiety lost in th' commotion.

Bull. An' why was that? Because the young are goin' who aren't already gone. Because there's ne'er a one, lad or lass, in th' disthrict between seventeen an' thirty. An' why are they gone?

Flagonson. To betther themselves, God help them! Even me own Judy an' Jack, up in Dublin, want me to settle them in London, where there's a betther openin', they say, God help them. Ay, an openin' into th' world that shuts them out from God!

Bull (*contemptuously*). Ay, so our clergy say. (*He throws back his head, and laughs contemptuously.*) Th' clergy! Ireland's a bird sanctuary for them. Priest-puffin island!

Flagonson (*with some remonstrance in his voice*). Now, Bull, now, Bull, dhraw it mild about th' clergy; not but I'd agree that it's hard to have an aysey mind with th' clergy pullin' out of us from all quarthers.

Bull. An' why th' hell haven't you got the spunk to fight some of their pirate pinchin'? What with their blue sisthers of th' poor, the white nuns of th' needy, th' brown sisthers of our crippled companions, we're rooked in th' mornin's, an' rooked at night, if our doors aren't bolted!

Flagonson (*losing his thoughts*). With church collectors runnin' along every road an' passable path, an' hoppin' over every stile, pattherin' at your doors like hailstones in a storm! With their 'The collector from Bona Mors, Mr. Farrell'; 'th' collector, Mr. Farrell, for th' new presbytery be the new church'; 'Mr. Farrell, th' collector for the Foreign Missions'; till a body's lightened of a lot he had to put away for a rainy day!

Bull (*remonstratively indignant*). Then why don't you fight it, man? (*He goes forward, and assumes a semi-fighting pose.*) Why don't you sthruggle against it, man? What ails you that you won't stand firm?

Flagonson (*half hesitatingly*). I will, I will, Bull; you'll see.

Bull (*scornfully*). You will, you will; I'll see, I'll see! When will I see? You've been sayin' that for years! Abnegate, I say, then, if you're a man, man.

Flagonson (*trying to be positive*). I will; I must. This pinchin' be th' priests of th' little we have is gettin' unconthrollable!

Bull. Isn't that what I'm after tellin' you! Priest-puffin island. An' it's not a shillin' they want, or even half-a-crown; oh, no; th' mineemus now asked from a poor thrader is a pound, if you please. And if a pound's given, they'll say with a blisterin' glance, 'If you're only givin' a pound, Mr. Farrell, you might as well make it one pound one'. Am I to be the one lone figure left standin', like a pillar without any support, to fight against this convulsion of givin' against our will? Is there ne'er a man but meself left in th' land? Are we to become only a scared an' scatthered crowd? Are you goin' to do anything, or are you not?

Flagonson (with heated resolution). I am! (*He bangs a tankard on the table.*) I will, I will; I must!

Bull (with scornful impatience). You must, you will! There's no surety in your tankard-dhrummin'. (*Savagely*) But will you, man; will you, will you?

> [*Two cyclists, a Young Man and a Young Woman, have come in from around the Tavern, pushing their bicycles along the road. He is simply dressed in tweeds and wears a tweed cap; his trouser-ends are thrust into his socks. She wears a dark jersey and green slacks. When they speak, they do so quickly, as if in a somewhat excited hurry. To Bull:*

Young Man (in quick excitement). How far from here, sir, is the remains of the Abbey of Ballyrellig?

Bull. Th' oul' graveyard with th' ruins in it is it you mean?

Young Man. It must be: th' one with the chapel of Saint Kurrakawn in it.

Young Woman (rapidly). A lovely crypt with groined arches, supported by lovely semi-columns, decorated with lovely foliage an' faces.

Bull. D'ye tell me that, now? Well, if what it is is what yous want, it's more'n fifteen miles farther on. But th' whole thing's lost, man, in thickets, brambles, an' briars.

Young Man (still speaking quickly). There's still a pathway to it, I'm told.

Bull. D'ye tell me that, now?

Young Woman. We simply must see it before we go away. It's just a dhream!

Bull. D'ye tell me that, now?

Young Man (to Young Woman). We'll want a meal first, dear. (*To Flagonson*) Can we have a fairly substantial one, sir?

Flagonson (with quiet assurance). Indeed, yous can; anything in reason; we're here to enthertain.

        [*He indicates the notice on the wall.*

   [*The Young Man and Young Woman wheel their bicycles towards the General Stores, and leave them leaning against the back wall.*

Young Man (glancing inquiringly at the Young Woman). A nice chop would make a good start?

Flagonson. A right royal start, if the chops were to be had, sir.

Young Woman (after a pause — to the Young Man). A few nice, lean rashers, Ned, would do just as well.

Flagonson. Ay, miss, an' fat ones, either, if there was any to be had. You don't expect us to kill a pig to provide yous with rashers, do yous?

Young Man (annoyed and disappointed). Well, what have you, then?

Flagonson. What about a boiled egg, a powerful cup o' tay, an' as much bread as you like to get down yous?

Young Woman (with a glance at the Young Man). That'll have to do, Ned.

Flagonson (indicating the Tavern door). In with yous, then, an' th' lady inside'll give yous all yous can conveniently want. *(The Young Man and Young Woman go rather slowly into the Tavern. To Bull)* Shockin' th' way the young demand things nowadays!

Bull. Their effervesacatin' spirits nowadays is incontrollable!

> [*Widda Machree appears around the back of the General Stores, walking along the road. She is a young woman of thirty. Her face is pale, well chiselled, and pure-looking. She wears a coloured scarf over her head, peasant-wise, so that the round of her face only is seen. A bright blue cloak draped from her shoulders half covers a black skirt and blouse. She wears black stockings and shoes. She is straightly built and slim, and has a semi-plaintive air, though this is occasionally changed into a humorous, half-cynical manner. She looks about her for a moment, and then speaks to the two men.*

Widda Machree (plaintively). I'm Widda Machree: me sweetheart died the day we were to wed, an' neighbours gave me the name I go by now. I'm in great throuble, gentlemen. I can't stay aysey by the big turf fire an' th' hearth swept clean. I have to thravel now along th' big bog road, because of a sin, gentlemen; an ugly, mortal sin, an' a mean one, too. Ochone, oh, ochone!

Flagonson. A bad burden to have on a conscience, ma'am.

Widda Machree. Ay; I'm but a wandherin' cloud o' conscience. There's ne'er a green glen left in Erin for me now. Never on Lady Day agin will I wear me dhress of speckled velvet, or sew the silver buckles on me shining shoon. O ochone, ochone!

Bull. No good'll come be dwellin' on it, ma'am.

Flagonson. You're th' lady was bargainin' with th' kilted gentleman over th' sale of your cow, aren't you?

Widda Machree. That thransaction was me undoin', gentlemen. I thought I could rise above th' temptation, but I sank below it. I'll sit down a second. (*She sits down on the bench.*) I'm tired searchin' for th' kilted gentleman. If he happens to pass by here, hold him till I call again. Kelly's th' name (*She gets up and swings round on her toes in a kind of dance, chanting:*)

> Has anybody here seen Kelly?
> K ee double ell y;
> Has anybody here seen Kelly,
> Kelly from the Isle of Man-an-aun!

I must settle accounts with him. Oh, ochone, I did a mean sin as well as a mortal one.

Bull. You looked sensible enough when I seen you bargainin' away with th' kilted man, opposite Trinity Church.

Widda Machree. At Trinity Church I met me doom, gentlemen. Givin' so much of me peace of mind to gain so little. Oh, miserere mei! I'll never go near th' church again till th' wrong's righted an' me soul feels free. But who am I tellin'? Sure you two musta often felt th' same way yourselves, for yous musta shot a gay lot o' rogueries into th' world in your time.

[*The quiet, matter-of-fact way that the last remark is made seems to stun the two men for a few moments, and they stand, silent, staring at her.*

Bull (*after a rather long pause*). I can tell you, ma'am, that the last remark you made is an entirely disilushunnary designation! There's ne'er a wisp of dishonesty to be found in either of our two firms!

Widda Machree. Don't crown your rogueries with a lie on top of them, good man. Didn't every soul I met comin' along here tell me yous were th' two most meritorious rogues in th' disthrict, an' that Canon Bullero commends all yous do because of the whack he gets out of it?

Flagonson (indignantly). Looka here, ma'am, I'm not anxious to have mortal sins any way adjacent to me respectable house; an' th' bench you're occupyin' is meant for customers only.

Widda Machree. Your hint is tellin' me it's time to go, sir.

Bull (coming nearer, and bending towards her till his face is close to hers — fiercely). An' with me fond farewell, let you tell all you meet that Bull Farrell hides no roguery undher the registered comfort of any priest's connivance, havin' refused to sanction th' givin' of ad libeetitum donations for th' period of sinny quaw non!

> [*Widda Machree rises from her seat, bows to the two men, and walks with slow dignity to the road. As she reaches it, the Young Man and the Young Woman come hurrying from the Tavern, both, evidently, in a deep state of indignation. They make for where their bicycles are. Mrs. Flagonson comes to the door to watch their departure. She is thirty-five, and not at all bad-looking. She is dressed neatly in a brown skirt and black bodice. A coloured cotton apron protects the skirt and the breast of the bodice.*

Young Man (holding his bicycle ready to go — angrily). A nest of daylight robbers! Five shillin's each for a crumb of bread, a cup of tea, and an egg wouldn't sit tight in a thimble! Daylight robbery!

Mrs. Flagonson (going over to Flagonson, and prodding him in the back with her forefinger). Not a word, mind you, Michael.

> [*She returns to the Tavern, and disappears within it.*

Young Man (sadly). Times have changed! When Brian Boru reigned, jewels an' costly garments could be left on the hedges without a soul thinkin' of touchin' them. But now!

Young Woman. I wondher what would Brian Boru think of it if he was. alive today!

Young Man (passionately). Or the Fenians before him, who set honour an' truth before comfort or safety. High hangin' to ye on a windy night, yeh bunch of incandescent thieves!

[*The Young Man and his companion go out indignantly, neither of the two men responding in any way. Widda Machree gazes fixedly at the two men for some moments during a short silence following the departure of the two young people. During the silence, the sound of coins jingling together is heard coming from Tavern and General Stores.*

Widda Machree (thoughtfully). A dangerous sound; a sound not to be mingled with the gentle jingle of the Mass bell. Take warnin' from me, gentlemen, who lost her virtue for a few lousy coins. Yous may go smilin' through th' world, gentlemen, but yous won't go smilin' through heaven. Let yous put more value into what yous give an' less into what yous get, before it's too late.

Bull (determinedly). Looka, you; go where you're goin' with less blather. We're not in th' same category, ma'am.

Widda Machree (after a slight pause). Looka, you; if sins were written on people's foreheads, th' two of yous would pull your caps well down over your eyes!

Flagonson. Please go, ma'am; we're reticent people, an' not interested in th' bouncing uttherance of things meant for the veiled ear of a priest.

Widda Machree. I'm goin', me lad. (*She starts on her way.*) I've warned yous. (*The sound of clinking coins, coming from the*

General Stores and the Tavern, which had faded, becomes clear again.) Aha, there's th' dangerous sound again, boys!

> [*She begins to sing, and again weaves herself into a dancing movement, wheeling round on her feet, and ending the chant just as she disappears around the Tavern.*

Widda Machree (*singing*):

> Jingle coins, jingle coins, jingle all the day.
> Count them all an' wrap them up an' tuck them safe away.
> Jingle coins, jingle on till life has pass'd away,
> Then change to foolish cries of woe upon th' judgement day!

Flagonson. Sounds a bit suspicious to me, Bull.

Bull. Suspicious? Didn't she tell her own story herself? A brazen bitch, Mick, an' a desiduous one, too!

Flagonson. Committin' mortal sin, mind you, with a go-boy in a sumptuous saffron kilt an' a gay green shawl.

Bull (*solemnly*). I always had me doubts about them laddos goin' about in kilts, Mick. On occasions of this kind, a kilt's an unpredictable garment for any man to be wearin'. (*He comes closer.*) She'll excite th' neighbours against us if she's not conthrolled. I shouldn't wondher if she was a Red!

Flagonson (*shocked*). No, no, God forbid! We must let the clergy know at once!

Bull (*throwing back his head for a guffaw*). Th' clergy! Priest-puffin island again. Not th' clergy, man, but th' polis!

> [*Barney O'Hay appears round the gable-end of the General Stores, and comes down from the road to Bull. He is a man of forty-five, thin and stringy. The evidence of continual toil and ever-present anxiety shows in the lines of his face which is seamed like a man of seventy.*

He is dressed in an old pair of khaki trousers, a shabby tweed coat, a little too short for him, and a well-worn waistcoat. A faded bowler hat covers his head, and his boots are patched. The one bright thing about him is a white, tall collar and brown tie which are symbols connecting him with the better-off farmers. He carries a blackthorn stick. He tries to walk briskly, but his steps are stiff; and his effort to smile cheerily but fills his face with a deeper gloom.

Barney (as he comes in). God save th' two men!

Flagonson
Bull } *(together — very coldly)*. You, too, O'Hay.

Barney (coming down to Bull as briskly as he can). Morra, Mr. Farrell — I've great news for you, so I have.

Bull (doubtfully). Huh, have you?

Barney (breezily). Ay have I; news'll cock y'up with pride an' pleasure.

> [*Flagonson has cocked his ears, though pretending to be indifferent.*

Bull (irritably). Well, out with it, if it's good news.

Barney (almost smacking his lips because of having something to say sure to please Farrell). Canon Whizzer's spreadin' it all over th' disthrict about you givin' him twenty pound this mornin'. Outa modesty, says he, Misther Farrell asked me to keep it secret; but, says he, such devotion is a thing to be told as an example to others. *(There is a dead silence. Seeing Bull glaring at him angrily, Barney looks at Flagonson, only to see him glaring angrily at Farrell. Haltingly)* I hope there's nothin' wrong.

Flagonson (to the world in general). God Almighty, a man never knows what he's shakin' hands with nowadays! What a quare sthress I'd have been in had I gone all out to provoke th' clergy! You'd think deception would have lessened its dimensions in this year of our anno domino!

[*Mrs. Flagonson comes from the Tavern and goes over to Flagonson.*

Mrs. Flagonson (*prodding Flagonson with her forefinger in the back*). Come, Michael, help feed th' chickens.

[*She returns to the Tavern, and Flagonson follows her meekly.*

Flagonson (*half to himself and half to the world — as he goes into the Tavern*). An' he only afther condemnin' a poor, decent woman for simply makin' a mistake! (*He throws his head backwards, and gives a loud, mocking guffaw.*) Priest-puffin island! D'ye get me, Mr. Bull Farrell!

Bull (*roughly and loudly to Barney*). Well, what d'ye want, blatherer?

Barney (*frightened*). I just came to get th' bag o' phosphates from you.

Bull. When you plank down a tenner of what you owe, you'll get it.

Barney (*half wailing*). I couldn't, I couldn't, Misther Farrell.

Bull. You couldn't, you couldn't! You sold your pigs, didn't you?

Barney (*plaintively*). Ah, sir, for next to nothin'. Th' kitchen leavin's I collected didn't make them prime. Th' slovenly bitches round here put tea-leaves, cabbage stalks, an' orange peel into it. How could any animal fatten itself on that stuff?

Bull. Gimme th' ten pounds you got for them, an' I'll let you have th' phosphate.

Barney. It was th' same with me acre o' hay — th' drouth banished all th' good out of it; an' th' acre o' spuds was mostly smalleens. I can't give th' tenner at once, sir.

Bull (almost shouting). Then get to hell outa here, then, if you can't!

> [*He turns away, goes into Stores, comes back to the door, where he stands, sourly smoking his pipe.*

> [*Barney goes back, abashed, to lean against the wall of the Stores, disconsolate.*

> [*Conroy and Cousins come in from the Tavern end; Conroy briskly, Cousins more slowly, a harassed look on his face. Conroy is middle-aged, Cousins about thirty years old. Conroy a man of a hundred and fifty acres, Cousins a man of twenty acres. Conroy wears cord breeches, Cousins corduroy ones; Conroy brown leggings, Cousins black ones, soiled with cow-dung; Conroy wears a sparkling bowler hat, Cousins a rumpled tweed hat. Both wear coats of dark-coloured cloth, and both carry sticks: Conroy's a fine, thick malacca cane, Cousins' a blackthorn. They come to the table.*

Cousins (following Conroy in). I just couldn't, Misther Conroy; I've taken fifteen pounds off already. They're fine beasts either for milkin' or beef; all-round animals, an' worth every penny of me first askin'.

Conroy (turning to look at Cousins pitifully). None o' them would win a fourth prize at a thin-stock show, man. I know a beast when I see one. It'll take an age of feedin' before them beasts is the kinda cattle you're dhreamin' they are.

> [*Bull, becoming interested in the bargaining, comes out from the door, and listens intently. Barney O'Hay gradually straightens up from the wall, and becomes interested too.*

Cousins. You prodded them with your stick till your arm ached, an' couldn't make a dint. A healthy herd they come from. There's growin' goodness in them beasts, I'm tellin' you.

Conroy (*laying a caressing hand on Cousins' arm*). Looka here, Cousins, I'm only thryin' to do a neighbour a good turn. I really don't want your beasts; they'll only be in th' way. Don't be too graspin', man! Here, take off another five pounds, an' I'll allow them to be mine.

Cousins (*shaking off Conroy's arm — indignantly*). Five pounds, is it? I'll dhrive them home first! (*He makes to go off, and reaches the road, where he pauses.*) Is that your final offer, Misther Conroy?

Conroy (*up to him*). Here, then — four pounds off: that, or nothin'!

Cousins (*coming back again*). Here, I'll split that as a favour — two off, an' that's me final word.

Conroy. Three, then. Is it a bargain? If not, I'm done. (*He holds a hand out to Cousins.*) Come on, man; put your hand there!

Cousins. Two ten, or nothin'. Here, two fifteen, then. Nothin' fairer. (*He holds a hand out.*) Before I go!

Conroy (*bringing his hand down on Cousins' with a loud smack*). Done! A dhrink for th' two of us. (*He raps on the table with his stick.*) Flagonson! Two whiskies!

> [*Flagonson brings out the drinks and leaves them on the table. Conroy and Cousins take them up to drink when Kelly from the Isle of Mananaun comes round by way of the Tavern. He is tall and straight. He wears a saffron kilt and a green shawl is draped from a shoulder. A black balmoral hat, with a green feather sticking up*

from it, covers his head. A silver pin-brooch shines in
his shawl. His face is pale and grave-looking, though
occasionally showing a satirical line in it. He halts on
the road, and looks towards the men.

Kelly (down to the men). Did any of yous, by any chance,
see a fine lady pass by? A lady with a fair face, gathered in a
little with grief, but with ne'er a hint o' guile in it?

Flagonson (with a wave of the hand — to Kelly). Go away, go
away, we're busy people here.

Kelly (musingly, as if to himself). A mortal sin torments my
coming in and my going out; a mortal sin and a mean one. (*To
the men*) Gentlemen, I must find the lady, and get back my
good name.

Flagonson (impatiently — with an angrier wave of his hand).
Go away, man; we're busy people here, I'm tellin' you!

Kelly. So I see; all bent down over the thought of gain.
(*A pause.*) Yous are all very close to hell now, gentlemen.
Take warnin' be me who gave too little for what I got.

Cousins (quickly). You bet th' poor lady's price down too
low?

Kelly. No, no; I gave her what she asked, but she asked too
little for what she gave.

Cousins (excited). Didja hear that, Misther Conroy? He
didn't give th' lady a fair price. A mortal sin — there's sense
in that, now.

Conroy (fiercely — to Cousins). Sense in it, you fool, because
it suits yourself.

Cousins. Th' gentleman's right — I didn't get half o' what I
gave was worth.

Kelly. It's a curse on us all, brother: givin' too little for what
we get.

Conroy (angrily — to Kelly). You must be th' boyo who th' Sergeant told me was spreadin' ideas about incitin' to discontentation everywhere. I can tell you, th' polis'll soon be on your tail!

Flagonson (to Kelly). Who are you, anyway? No-one even knows your name.

Kelly (doing the dance the Widda did, but turning round the reverse way — lilting):

> Th' name I'm called is Kelly,
> K ee double ell y;
> Th' name I'm called is Kelly,
> Kelly from the Isle of Mananaun!

Go on, gentlemen, with your gettin' of gain while the great big world keeps turnin'.

Conroy (jeeringly). G'wan, you, an' find your lady, an' cuddle her into agreein' with your curious theologicality.

Bull (maliciously). Lady is it? Seems like she's a one would settle down in a ditch with a donor.

Kelly (calmly). Aha, so you've bad minds along with th' love of gain. You thry to pin on others th' dirty decorations that may be hangin' on your own coats. (*He points, one after the other at Conroy, Bull, and Flagonson. Lilting*):

> Who were you with last night?
> Who were you with last night?
> Will you tell your missus when you go home
> Who you were with last night?

Flagonson (in anguished indignation). This is more than a hurt to us: this hits at the decency of the whole nation!

Kelly (pointing his forefinger straight at Conroy). Do you go to Mass?

Conroy (*sputtering*). Do I go to Mass? Of course I go to Mass, sir!

Kelly. An' don't you feel odd an' outa place there, thinking of gains in the week gone, and th' gains of th' week to come?

Conroy. Me outa place there! What th' hell d'ye mean, man?

Barney (*bursting out from his somewhat obscure corner, and standing forth to confront Kelly*). I'll not stand here to hear Misther Conroy insulted! I'll have you know Misther Conroy's chairman of the Catholic Young Men's Society; that Misther Conroy's name's down for th' medal of St. Silvesther; that Misther Conroy's a Grand Knight of St. Columbanus; an' that Misther Conroy's a particular friend of Monsignor Moymelligan's!

Kelly. Aha, but is Misther Conroy a particular friend of th' saints?

Conroy (*furiously*). I'm not goin' to stand here an' see th' saints insulted; an' I'll not stand here, either, to listen to your unannounceable mystheries that would shear all companionable manners from our business consortations!

Cousins (*soothingly*). Aysey, Misther Conroy; aysey!

Conroy (*raging*). Good God, what are we payin' the Civic Guards for! Where are th' loafers hidin'? Is a man like me to be hunted into an indetermination rage by th' unsponsored, piseudo religiosity of a kilted bum! I'll soon put th' law on his heels! (*He rushes on to the road past Kelly, then turns to face him.*) You musta come from some quare place, I'm thinkin', to be makin' a mock of all the things we hold so sacred. I'll settle you!

[*He makes to rush off behind the Tavern. Kelly points a forefinger towards his back, and emits a sharp, short whistle, and Conroy suddenly stops dead in his rush,*

and stands stiff, one leg stretched out before the other,
having stopped in the act of finishing a step forward. The
others look on with amazement and some alarm.

Kelly (*down to the surprised men — somewhat humorously*).
See? A pointing finger can stop him in his stride. As long as it
points, he stays put. But a stretched arm would soon grow
tired, so I'll send him off on his errand of mercy.

[*He again emits a short, sharp whistle, lowers his arm, and*
Conroy resumes his rush, apparently unaware of what
has happened. The others, a little frightened, draw
gradually away from Kelly, towards the protection of
the houses — Flagonson and Cousins to the Tavern, and
Bull and Barney towards the General Stores, till they
are half hidden standing in the entrance to each.

Kelly. Don't be slinkin' off like as if yous had murdhered
Nellie O'Flaherty's beautiful dhrake. (*The clink of coins is*
heard again in Tavern and Stores.) Aha, that's how th' harp o'
Tara sounds today! What's it playin'? (*The tune of 'Jingle*
Bells' is softly heard.) I am in my sleep, an' don't waken me. A
signature song! (*Going slowly away behind the General Stores,*
lilting as he crosses:)

Jingle coins, jingle coins, jingle all th' day,
Jingle them at night again, for coins have come to stay.
Jingle coins till silent Death comes in his frozen sleigh
To gather yous an' all your coins, an' jingle yous away!

[*He disappears around the back of the General Stores. The*
rest, by this time, are hidden within Tavern and Stores,
their heads only peeping out around the jambs of the
doorways.

Flagonson (*peeping out from behind the door*). Is he gone?

Cousins (*coming out a little way from the Tavern door*). Yis.
No sign of him now.

Bull (*coming out of the Stores*). We should have faced him out; should've stood up to him; defied him. We're not worums!

Flagonson (*decisively*). No, Bull, no. There was magic in that figure, man. When he pointed at me and asked me who I was with last night, I felt it slippin' up an' down me spine.

Cousins (*timidly*). All th' same, he said one thing worth thinkin' of when he told us it was a mortal sin to give too little for a thing you're buyin'.

Barney (*assertively*). Misther Conroy was right; he musta come from some quare place, for to bring in th' topic of religion outa hours shows a quare mind. (*He suddenly listens.*) I hear a step. Someone's comin' again.

> [*They all make for Tavern and Stores, and try to peep round the doorways towards the road. The Sergeant comes stealthily in along the road, looking fearfully to right and left. He comes down till he is close to the Tavern.*

Sergeant (*in towards the Tavern — in a loud whisper*). Misther Farrell, are yous there? (*He hurries across to the Stores, and whispers towards the door.*) Misther Flagonson, are yous there?

> [*The four men, affected by the stealthiness of the Sergeant, become stealthy too. They come out of Tavern and Stores to gather round him, heads bent inwards towards each other, and shoulders crouched low.*

Flagonson. What is it, Sergeant? What has you goin' about gathered up like a cod in a pot?

Sergeant (*warningly*). Hush! Thry to feel unconscious of all wrong-doin'. Thry to look, not like the gaums yous are, but like innocent ones.

Bull (*impatiently*). What sorta talk's this, Sergeant?

Sergeant. Hush, I'm sayin'. Not so loud. Th' west's asleep. Th' Inspector says to me, Killdooey, he says, find out th' antecedents of th' person.

Flagonson. Ah, the antecedents.

Sergeant. An' no names mentioned, Sergeant, says he, for identification might prove dangerous. (*He suddenly looks down at each arm.*) Now which is me right arm an' which is me left one?

Bull (*indicating it*). That's your right one. Godamit, man, don't you know one arm from t'other yet?

Sergeant (*not noticing Bull's remark*). Folly it up to Carlow, he says.

Barney. Folly what up to Carlow, man?

Sergeant (*whispering low*). Th' person, sir. Folly th' person, says th' Inspector, even if th' person goes up to Carlow.

⟩ *Cousins.* We don't get th' dhrift of what you're dhrivin' at, Sergeant.

Sergeant (*seizing Flagonson by the arm*). Looka, Bull Farrell, I love a lassie. D'ye know?

Flagonson (*bewildered*). Yis, yis, I know.

Sergeant (*lilting*):
   A bonnie Hielan' lassie:
(*In a loud and positive burst of song:*)
   She's as pure as th' lily in th' dell!

Flagonson: Yis, yis, you can tell us about that again. What's throublin' us is what's throublin' you?

Sergeant (*dreamily*). Ay, ay; it's th' person who's goin' about dividin' th' people into fightin' over what th' person says.

Cousins (*impatiently*). An' what, in God's name, is th' person actually sayin', Sergeant?

Sergeant (*dreamily*). Th' person's in th' throes of a mortal sin for sellin' a cow to someone, an' askin' too much for it, so th' person's sayin' ask less than you'd like to get for a thing you're sellin'.

Cousins (*indignantly*). No, no; that's against all law an' livability! Where's th' freedom our poor boys died to get, if a body daren't ask for what he wants for a thing he's sellin'? You're mixin' things up, Sergeant; th' kilted person passin' here said th' very opposite!

Sergeant. Th' skirted person, you mean?

Cousins. Th' kilted person, I'm sayin'.

Flagonson (*excitedly*). We forgot th' first one!

Sergeant. Which first one, what first one?

Flagonson. A person opposin' in appearance th' person we have in mind now.

Sergeant (*putting a hand to his brow to help in very deep thought*). Then th' person has two presenceses. (*He pauses, then stretches out his right arm in front of him.*) We'll get to th' bottom of it, sure's this is me left arm!

Barney (*in a whisper — to Bull*). Is he dhrunk or what?

[*Barney has been watching the Sergeant for some time with intensity, and now moves very gradually away from the group, keeping still a watch on the Sergeant.*

Sergeant (*dreamily*). Comin' through th' rye to here, I felt shaky. I thried to whistle, but no sound came to me assistance. I sucked in an' I blew out, but ne'er a single sound came to me assistance. (*He puts his face close to Bull's, and whispers*) Looka, Inspector, I feel like — what do I feel like? I feel like th' man who sthruck O'Hara! (*He takes his face away from Bull's, and begins to sing, accompanying, at first, with so sudden a sway that the others (except Barney) catch hold of him and are forced to join in the movement. The Sergeant goes on accompanying the words with the movements which the words seem to suggest (at times, somewhat violent), and those clinging to him are forced to move with him. Singing and carrying on mime movements:)*

First we mopp'd th' floor with him,
Dragg'd him up an' down th' stairs;

Then we had another go, undher tables, over chairs.
Such a sight you never saw —
Before he'd time to say his prayers,

Rags an' bones were all we left
Of th' man who sthruck O'Hara!

Barney (shrinking back towards the Stores). God Almighty, th' fella's touched!

Flagonson (agonised). Aw, pull yourself together, Sergeant!

[*The Sergeant, with an effort, straightens himself as if for parade. Outside, the voice of Widda Machree is heard lilting quietly the chorus of 'I Know Where I'm Goin''.*

Widda Machree (lilting, outside):

I know where I'm goin',
And I know who's goin' with me;
I know who I love,
But th' dear knows who I'll marry!

[*Widda Machree comes in from the back of the General Stores. The men sense her presence, and stand tense in a semicircle together, their backs to the road along which the Widda is walking. She looks down towards them. Just as she comes in, the Sergeant wilts away again, crouching and tense as the rest are.*

Bull (in a whisper — to the Sergeant). Now or never, Sergeant, thry to pull yourself together!

Widda Machree. God save yous all. I feel me journey's endin'. (*She lilts and wheels around in a kind of dance:*)

> Has anybody here seen Kelly?
> Kay ee double ell y;
> Has anybody here seen Kelly?
> Kelly from th' Isle of Mananaun!

(*Down to the men*) Have yous seen a spirit, or what, yous are so silent? Have yous no music in yous save the din of the market-place?

Bull (*whispering passionately to the Sergeant*). Now, Sergeant, up, an' answer her!

Widda Machree. No picture in your minds but a warrant for an arrest, or a bill demandin' pay for goods delivered?

Sergeant (*in a whisper to Bull*). I have to wait for reinforcements!

Widda Machree. You is neither fit for heaven nor to take th' floor at Phil the Fluther's Ball! (*From around the back of the Stores, opposite to where the Widda Machree stands, Kelly comes. He halts when he sees her, and both gaze silently at each other for some moments. Then each holds out arms to the other as they come close.*) My brother!

Kelly. My sisther! (*Offering her a purse*) Take all I kept from you; and take th' cow back, too, for I gave less than I should when I was buying.

Widda Machree (*offering him a purse*). Take back all you gave, an' keep th' cow, for I asked more than I should when I was sellin'.

Widda Machree }
Kelly } (*together*). Forgive!

[*They enter into each other's arms.*

Kelly. More than sisther!

Widda Machree. More than brother!

> [*A blast from a police whistle is heard; the Sergeant leaps to life, and Conroy, followed by two Civic Guards, rushes in, the 1st Civic Guard still blowing his whistle. They halt for a second when they see the two embracing, and look on for a second.*

Conroy (*excitedly*). There they are — the ruffians! Surround them; hold them tight!

1st C. Guard (*waving papers in the air*). We've got th' warrants indictin' them for breaches of th' peace.

2nd C. Guard (*waving papers in the air*). An' a full-blown certificate from Doctor Simples showin' neither of them non compos mentis.

Flagonson		Handcuff them!
Bull	*(in unison)*	Put them behind bars at once.
Barney		Solitary confinement for th' pair o' them.
Cousins		Yis, yis; th' sight of them unsettles us.

> [*Widda Machree and Kelly are handcuffed, the Sergeant and the 1st Civic Guard placing themselves beside Kelly, while the 2nd Civic Guard takes charge of Widda Machree.*

Conroy. Go on, Sergeant, dhrag them off before we hear more of their lies, one sayin' 'Give more when you're buyin'', an' th' other sayin' 'Ask less when you're sellin''.

Kelly (*to Conroy*). Th' sayin's, sir, are but two sides of the same truth.

Conroy (*angrily*). Will you take away th' deludherin' louser, Sergeant, an' not be lettin' him go on talkin'!

Kelly (*pointing to the blasted trees*). Soon yous'll all be no more than are these two barren, deadened trees. Then when yous are silent stiffs, others will count your coins.

Sergeant (laying a hand on Kelly's shoulder). Come on, me man, to where you'll be cured into seein' things as we all see them.

2nd C. Guard (laying a hand on Widda Machree's shoulder). An' you, me woman, come along to where your poor mind'll be mended.

Kelly (to Widda Machree). It is time to go, sisther.

Widda Machree (to Kelly). It is time to go, brother.

Kelly (embracing and kissing her). Goodbye, fair sweetheart.

Widda Machree (kissing him). Goodbye, my love.

[*The Sergeant, followed by the 1st Civic Guard, leads out Kelly by way of the Stores; the 2nd Civic Guard leads out Widda Machree by way of the Tavern. As they go, Kelly and the Widda Machree perform their wheeling dance they did before, while Kelly says his last farewell, and Widda Machree says hers.*

Kelly (wheeling quietly in his semi-dance, as he goes out):
> Goodbye to holy souls left here,
> Goodbye to man an' fairy;

Widda Machree (wheeling quietly in her semi-dance, as she goes out):
> Goodbye to all of Leicester Square,
> An' th' long way to Tipperary.

Conroy (taking off his hat and mopping his head with a big handkerchief). What a dispicable pair! Thank th' holy saints that that danger's past. (*To Cousins*) Now let us settle up in peace.

[*He takes a wallet from his pocket, is about to open it, when he cocks an ear to listen.*

[*The tune of 'Jingle Coins', accompanied by voices singing the words, is heard, sung and played softly, as if coming from a great distance.*

Voices (with accompaniment):

Jingle coins, jingle coins, jingle all the day,
Jingle them at night again, for coins have come to stay.
Jingle them till silent Death comes in his frozen sleigh
To gather you and all your coins, and jingle yous away!

Conroy. Is that th' sound of singin' somewhere I hear?

Cousins. Yis; seems to be something familiar.

Bull. The Civic Guards cod-actin' in th' barracks down th' road.

[*Conroy opens his wallet as he stands by the table, and is about to count out notes, when the Sergeant and 1st Civic Guard rush in from behind the Stores. They are in a great state of excitement.*

Sergeant (to the others — breathless). Did he go this way? We seen him flash by here. Are yous dumb? Answer!

Conroy. Who, who, man?

Sergeant. Kelly from th' Isle of Mananaun. Just slid out o' th' handcuffs, out of our hold, an' was gone!

[*The 2nd Civic Guard rushes in, panic-stricken, from around the Tavern.*

2nd C. Guard (hysterically). Did she go this way? I seen her flashin' by. Goddamnit, answer!

Conroy. Who, who, man?

2nd C. Guard. Th' lady, th' hussy. Just slid outa me grip, an' was gone!

Conroy (with a furious shout). Then go afther them an' get them, you blasted fools!

[*The Sergeant and the 1st Civic Guard rush out in one direction, the 2nd Civic Guard in the other.*

[*The tune of 'Jingle Coins' played on trumpet and drum becomes loud and clear now, and all stand tensely to listen. The two barren trees in the background suddenly flush with blossom, foliage, and illuminated fruit.*

Bull (*listening*). They're mockin' us in some place or another; in some place unknown.

Cousins (*excitedly pointing to the trees*). Look, looka th' threes!

Barney (*falling on his knees*). Jayayus, a miracle!

Cousins (*falling on his knees*). They musta been saints!

[*Bull and Flagonson now fall on their knees, too, and all face towards the glowing trees.*

[*After a few moments, Mrs. Flagonson appears at the Tavern door, goes over to Flagonson, taking no notice of what has happened, and prods her husband in the back with her forefinger.*

[*The glowing trees begin to fade as soon as Mrs. Flagonson prods her husband in the back.*

Mrs. Flagonson (*prodding her husband*). Come in, Michael, an' help me tot up th' takin's.

[*Without a word, Flagonson gets up and follows his wife into the Tavern, and the glowing trees fade away utterly, becoming dead and barren again. The others rise a few moments afterwards, stand still for a second or so, then look sheepishly at each other.*

Conroy (*roughly to Cousins*). Come on in, an' let's settle up in quietness for th' scrawls o' cattle I was a fool to buy.

[*He goes into the Tavern.*

Bull (*to Barney*). No use o' you stayin' here. Bring me th' tenner, or you'll get no phosphate from me.

[*He goes into the Stores.*

[*Barney turns slowly away and makes for the road to go home, and on the way out Cousins stops him with a question.*

Cousins (*to the dejected Barney*). Didja see anything, Mr. O'Hay? I wondher what was it I seen?

Barney. If I seen anything, an' if you seen anything, what was seen was only an halleelucination!

[*He goes dejectedly on his way, and Cousins goes slowly into the Tavern.*

END OF THE PLAY

HAS ANYBODY HERE SEEN KELLY?

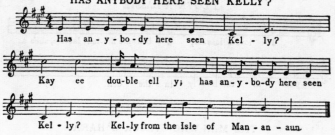

Has an-y-bo-dy here seen Kel - ly?
Kay ee dou-ble ell y; has an-y-bo-dy here seen
Kel - ly? Kel-ly from the Isle of Man-an-aun.

JINGLE COINS, JINGLE COINS

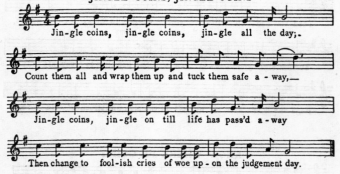

Jin-gle coins, jin-gle coins, jin-gle all the day;
Count them all and wrap them up and tuck them safe a-way,—
Jin-gle coins, jin-gle on till life has pass'd a-way
Then change to fool-ish cries of woe up-on the judgement day.

WHO WERE YOU WITH LAST NIGHT

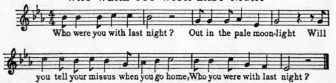

Who were you with last night? Out in the pale moon-light Will
you tell your missus when you go home, Who you were with last night?

I LOVE A LASSIE

I love a lass-ie, a bon-nie Hie-lan' las-sie, she's as pure as the li-ly in the dell.

THE MAN WHO STRUCK O'HARA

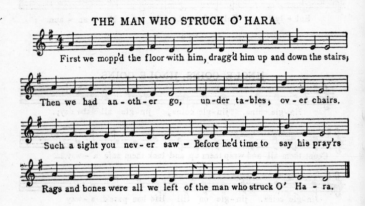

First we mopp'd the floor with him, dragg'd him up and down the stairs;
Then we had an-oth-er go, un-der ta-bles, ov-er chairs.
Such a sight you nev-er saw — Before he'd time to say his pray'rs
Rags and bones were all we left of the man who struck O' Ha-ra.

I KNOW WHERE I'M GOING

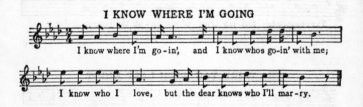

I know where I'm go-in', and I know whos go-in' with me;
I know who I love, but the dear knows who I'll mar-ry.

*Printed in Great Britain by Richard Clay (The Chaucer Press), Ltd.,
Bungay, Suffolk*